Reading FORWARD

INTERMEDIATE 1

INTERMEDIATE 1

Series Editors Bin-na Yang, Dong-sook Kim

Project Editors Jung-ah Lee, Mina Song, Mi-youn Woo, Jee-young Song, Jin-young Song, Sung-ho Jun, Seol-mee Lee

Contributing Writers Patrick Ferraro, Henry John Amen IV, John Boswell, Robert Vernon, Alicja Serafin, Keeran Murphy, Peter Morton

Illustrators Seol-hee Kim, Hyun-jin Choi, Hyo-sil Lee, Da-som Kim

Design Ho-hyun Bang, Hyun-jung Jang, Yeon-joo Kim

Editorial Designer In-sun Lee

Sales Ki-young Han, Kyung-koo Lee, In-gyu Park, Cheol-gyo Jeong, Nam-jun Kim, Nam-hyung Kim, Woo-hyun Lee

Marketers Hye-sun Park, Yeo-jin Kim, Ji-won Lee

Copyright © 2015 by NE Neungyule, Inc.

First Printing 15 June 2015

12th Printing 15 November 2022

ISBN 979-11-253-0798-3 53740

INTRODUCTION

★
★
★

Reading Forward is a six-level series of three progressive steps: Basic, Intermediate, and Advanced. Based on the essential needs of young students, the series focuses on a specific goal: expanding vocabulary and knowledge. This goal guides all of the content and activities in the series. The first step of the series will enlarge vocabulary, and the later steps will increase knowledge. Thus, the series will eventually help students improve their reading comprehension.

Each book of Reading Forward is composed of 20 units. The number of words used in each reading passage is as follows.

Step 3
Reading Forward
Advanced
for Knowledge
1 : 240 – 260 words
2 : 260 – 280 words

Step 2
Reading Forward
Intermediate
for Vocabulary & Knowledge
1 : 200 – 220 words
2 : 220 – 240 words

Step 1
Reading Forward
Basic
for Vocabulary
1 : 150 – 170 words
2 : 170 – 190 words

Key Features of Reading Forward Series

– Current, high-interest topics are developed in an easy way so that students can understand them. These subjects can hold their attention and keep them motivated to read forward.

– Comprehension checkup questions presented in the series are based on standardized test questions. These can help students prepare for English tests at school, as well as official English language tests.

– Each unit is designed to expand vocabulary and knowledge by presenting newly created sections: English Dictionary, Encyclopedia Contents related to the main topic. Students will be intrigued by this intellectual content and eventually build the basics of improved reading comprehension.

FORMAT

Before Reading

The question before each passage allows students to think about the topic by relating it to their lives. It also helps students become interested in the passage before reading it.

Reading

This part serves as the main passage of the unit, and it explains an intriguing and instructive topic in great depth. As students progress through the book, the content of these passages becomes more and more substantial.

Reading Comprehension

The reading is followed by different types of questions, which test understanding of the passage. The various types of questions focus on important reading skills, such as understanding the main idea and organization of the passage, identifying details, and drawing inferences.

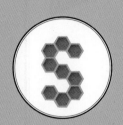

Strategic Summary / Organizer

Each unit includes a strategic summary or organizer of the main reading passage. It gives students a better understanding of the important points and organization of the passage. These exercises focus on further development of effective reading comprehension skills.

Knowledge Expanding

Each unit provides one of three different forms in Knowledge Expanding: Encyclopedia Contents, English Dictionary, and a further reading passage. These are related to the topic of the main passage, and thus it allows students to explore the topic in depth and expand their vocabulary.

Vocabulary Review

A review of the key vocabulary concludes each unit. Three types of exercises test understanding of new words: matching definitions, identifying synonyms and antonyms, and completing sentences with the correct words in context.

TABLE OF CONTENTS

★　★　★　★　★

Reading Forward

Before Reading

How would you make the Olympic Games more enjoyable and interesting?

The Indigenous Olympics

Everyone in the world enjoys the Olympic Games. But in Brazil, some people get more excited about another special event — the Indigenous Olympics. It was first organized by Brazilian soccer legend Pele in 1996. Every year, thousands of people from over 40 tribes get together to take part in the

5　games.

　　Like the Olympic Games, the Indigenous Olympics start with a fantastic opening ceremony. ① During the ceremony, all the tribes enter the stadium in a parade. ② They sing and dance in traditional costumes, including grass skirts and animal skin jewelry. ③ Some people don't like to wear

10　traditional costumes. ④ At the end of the ceremony, a torch is lit and an amazing fireworks display follows. The games last a week, and athletes play _____(A)_____, such as swimming, tug-of-war, spear throwing, canoeing, and archery. The highlight is a tree-log relay race, where runners run around with a 200-pound tree trunk on their shoulder!

15　　　Athletes are not trained for the games, so there are often funny episodes. In one race, a runner kept running past the finish line. Another time, some of the winners didn't show up at the victory stand to receive their medals. They had already left the stadium to enjoy a festival outside! In fact, medals and rankings aren't important to them. But all the tribes happily

20　attend the games and celebrate their coming together!

1 What is the best title for the passage?

  a. The World's Largest Festival

  b. A Special Sports Event in Brazil

  c. The History of Native Brazilians

  d. Different Kinds of Olympic Sports

2 Which sentence is NOT needed in the passage?

  a. ①   *b.* ②   *c.* ③   *d.* ④

3 What is the best choice for blank (A)?

  a. only the tribes' own sports

  b. modern and traditional sports

  c. the most dangerous sports in the world

  d. the same sports as those of the regular Olympics

4 Why didn't some of the winners appear at the victory stand?

_____

5 What is NOT mentioned about the Indigenous Olympics?

  a. When the games first started

  b. What people do during the opening ceremony

  c. How long the games last

  d. How many sports are played during the games

6 Write T if the statement is true or F if it's false.

  1) The Indigenous Olympics are held every four years.

  2) The Indigenous Olympics help celebrate the unity between tribes.

STRATEGIC SUMMARY

Fill in the blanks with the correct words.

Every year, the Indigenous Olympics are held in Brazil. In some ways, they are _____ to the regular Olympic Games: There is a big opening ceremony, a torch is lit, and some of the same sports are played. But in other ways, they are very _____. For example, the Indigenous Olympics include some _____ sports, such as tug-of-war and tree-log relay racing. Also, athletes do not _____ for the games, and they don't think rankings and medals are important. The Indigenous Olympics are held so that tribes can have fun and _____ their coming together!

> receive   similar   celebrate   different   train   traditional

★ EXPANDING KNOWLEDGE ★

Encyclopedia Contents: Olympic Games

1. Ancient Olympics
2. Modern Olympics
   2.1 1896 Games: the first Olympics
3. Changes
   3.1 Winter games
   3.2 Paralympics: for disabled athletes
   3.3 Youth games
4. Symbols
   4.1 Olympic rings
4. Ceremonies
   4.1 Opening
   4.2 Closing
   4.3 Medal presentation
5. Sports
   5.1 Summer games: 28 sports
   5.2 Winter games: 7 sports
6. Host nations and cities
7. International Olympic Committee (IOC)

1 Write the correct highlighted word next to its definition.

1) belonging to a time long ago in history: _____

2) a country or city that holds a special event: _____

3) unable to use a part of one's body properly because of injury or illness: _____

2 Write T if the statement is true or F if it's false.

1) The first modern Olympic Games were held at the end of the 19th century.

2) The Olympic Games program consists of over 40 sports.

VOCABULARY REVIEW

A Write the correct word next to its definition.

archery	athlete	torch	celebrate	trunk

1 the sport of shooting arrows: _____

2 the thick central part of a tree: _____

3 a stick with material at its top that is burned to give light: _____

4 to do something special in order to show that an event is important: _____

B Find the word that has a similar meaning to the underlined word.

1 I'm going to Brazil to take part in a festival.

  a. deal with   *b.* depend on   *c.* account for   *d.* participate in

2 His dream is to organize a rock band with his high school friends.

  a. join   *b.* help   *c.* meet   *d.* establish

C Choose the best word to complete each sentence.

1 They went to the _____ to watch a soccer game.

  a. tribe   *b.* costume   *c.* stadium   *d.* score

2 We had many funny _____ during the last trip.

  a. freedoms   *b.* episodes   *c.* ceremonies   *d.* medals

3 Jay was upset that I didn't _____ for his dinner party.

  a. warm up   *b.* cheer up   *c.* set up   *d.* show up

4 Our team is in fifth place in the world _____.

  a. rankings   *b.* messages   *c.* practice   *d.* teamwork

The Croissant

If you go to France, you'll see many people eating *crescent-shaped pastries. This soft, crispy, buttery food is called a "croissant," which means "crescent" in French. It is one of the most popular kinds of bread in the world.

5 As its name is French, many people think it comes from France. But some say it actually comes from Austria. In 1683, Austria was at war with Turkey. (①) After several months of attacking, the Turks tried to dig an underground tunnel to get into Vienna. (②) Just in time, some bakers working in a basement heard the sounds of digging. (③) To celebrate the victory, the bakers made pastries in the shape of the crescent that they had 10 seen on the Turkish flag. (④) When the Austrians ate them, they felt like they were biting the Turks!

There is also a story about _____(A)_____. It is said that Marie Antoinette, the Austrian princess who married King Louis XVI, brought croissants to France about 100 years later. Maybe she liked croissants too 15 much to live without them!

However, many people doubt the truth of these stories because the croissant as we know it today didn't appear in any books until 1906. But even though its beginnings are uncertain, there is no doubt that the croissant is a symbol of 20 French culture today.

*crescent: a curved shape that is wider in the middle and pointed at the ends

1 **What is the passage mainly about?**

a. The origin of the croissant

b. The popularity of the croissant

c. The war between Austria and Turkey

d. The Austrian princess, Marie Antoinette

2 **Where would the following sentence best fit?**

> Thanks to the bakers, the Austrian army destroyed the tunnel and defeated their enemy.

a. ①   b. ②   c. ③   d. ④

3 **What is the best choice for blank (A)?**

a. the training of bakers

b. the power of French kings

c. the croissant's original design

d. the croissant's introduction to France

4 **Why are the stories of the croissant often doubted by people?**

_____

5 **What is NOT mentioned about the croissant?**

a. What its name means

b. Where it came from

c. When it was first made

d. How it is baked

6 **Write T if the statement is true or F if it's false.**

1) Austrian bakers dug an underground tunnel to attack the Turks.

2) It is believed that the croissant was made to celebrate victory in a war.

Fill in the blanks with the correct words.

Although the croissant is known as a popular French pastry, some say it actually comes from Austria. In 1683, during a war between Austria and Turkey, Austrian bakers _____ that the Turks were trying to attack Vienna by building an underground tunnel. Thanks to the bakers, the army was able to _____ the tunnel and defeat the enemy. To celebrate the _____, the bakers made pastries in the shape of the crescent on the Turkish flag. Many years later, Marie Antoinette is said to have brought the croissant to France. Since then, it has become a _____ of French culture.

crispy	victory	symbol	destroy	discovered

★ EXPANDING KNOWLEDGE ★

Encyclopedia Contents: Bread

1. History

2. Grains for bread
   2.1 Wheat
   2.2 Rye
   2.3 Oats
   2.4 Corn

3. Main ingredients
   3.1 Flour
   3.2 Eggs and butter
   3.3 Sugar and salt
   3.4 Yeast

4. Nutrients
   4.1 Carbohydrates
   4.2 Vitamins and minerals
   4.3 Dietary fiber

5. Traditional Breads
   5.1 Indian ⋯ naan
   5.2 French ⋯ baguette
   5.3 German ⋯ pretzel
   5.4 Scottish ⋯ scone
   5.5 Mexican ⋯ tortilla
   5.6 North American ⋯ cornbread

1 Write the correct highlighted word next to its definition.

1) healthy substances taken into the body: _____

2) related to old cultural customs or beliefs: _____

3) a white powder made by grinding grains: _____

2 Write T if the statement is true or F if it's false.

1) Salt as well as sugar is used to make bread.

2) Bread does not contain any dietary fiber.

VOCABULARY REVIEW

A Write the correct word next to its definition.

introduction	bite	basement	attack	dig

1 to make a hole in the ground: _____

2 to cut something with one's teeth: _____

3 to take military action against enemies in a war: _____

4 a room or area that is below the level of the ground: _____

B Find the word that has a similar meaning to the underlined word.

1 It is <u>uncertain</u> how many people are needed for the project.

    a. exact   *b.* serious   *c.* unclear   *d.* curious

2 I'm very disappointed that my team was <u>defeated</u> by one point.

    a. changed   *b.* beaten   *c.* failed   *d.* stopped

C Choose the best word to complete each sentence.

1 My favorite actor will _____ in the next scene.

    a. appear   *b.* happen   *c.* promote   *d.* encourage

2 The entire city was totally _____ by the earthquake.

    a. monitored   *b.* respected   *c.* developed   *d.* destroyed

3 I _____ that I can finish this report. There is not enough time.

    a. think   *b.* doubt   *c.* prevent   *d.* predict

4 This _____ cookie is not only delicious but also easy to make.

    a. sudden   *b.* crispy   *c.* quick   *d.* violent

Uncle Sam

I WANT YOU
FOR U.S. ARMY
NEAREST RECRUITING STATION

Have you ever seen a tall man in a top hat and clothes that look like the American flag? That's Uncle Sam, a famous American icon. So where did he come from?

During the *War of 1812, a meatpacker named Sam provided the U.S. Army with meat. The barrels he sent were marked U.S., for the United States. However, the soldiers joked that the letters stood for Uncle Sam. When people heard this story, they began thinking of "Uncle Sam" as a nickname for the United States.

The first image of Uncle Sam appeared in a political cartoon in the 1830s. (①) But he didn't look like he does today. (②) After his first appearance, his image changed from picture to picture. (③) Thus, he became a tall, thin man with a beard. (④) Also, he usually wore a *stars-and-stripes suit and top hat. But the most famous

20 image of Uncle Sam is from World War I army recruiting posters. In these posters, he is staring and pointing his finger at the viewer, with the phrase "I Want You for U.S. Army" written beneath him. This picture made him
_____(A)_____ .

Today, this image of Uncle Sam is often used in American popular

25 culture. For example, a famous baseball team, the New York Yankees, uses Uncle Sam's hat in their team logo.

*War of 1812: a war between the U.S. and England
*stars-and-stripes: referring to the national flag of the U.S.

1 What is the best title for the passage?

    a. Uncle Sam: A Symbol of the U.S.

    b. Uncle Sam: A Hero of the Civil War

    c. Uncle Sam: The Best Baseball Player Ever

    d. Uncle Sam: A Greatly Loved Cartoon Character

2 How did people respond when they heard the soldiers' joke about the letters "U.S."?

_____

3 Where would the following sentence best fit?

> Around the time of the Civil War, Uncle Sam was drawn to resemble President Abraham Lincoln.

    a. ①   *b.* ②   *c.* ③   *d.* ④

4 What is the best choice for blank (A)?

    a. everybody's friend

    b. as famous as a movie star

    c. look less like a real person

    d. a well-known national symbol

5 What is NOT mentioned about the Uncle Sam icon?

    a. Where it came from

    b. Who drew it first

    c. How its image has changed

    d. What the most famous version is

6 Write T if the statement is true or F if it's false.

    1) The first image of Uncle Sam looked like Abraham Lincoln.

    2) The image of Uncle Sam is still used in American culture today.

Fill in the blanks with the correct words.

Uncle Sam	— A famous American _____

The origin	• It was based on Sam, who _____ the U.S. Army with meat.
The image	• Uncle Sam was first drawn in the 1830s. • He was drawn to _____ Abraham Lincoln around the time of the Civil War. • His most _____ image appeared during WW I.
Today	• The New York Yankees use his hat in their logo.

provided	president	icon	popular	look like

★ EXPANDING KNOWLEDGE ★

WHO'S ABSENT?

Just as the U.S. has Uncle Sam, Britain has John Bull as its national symbol. John Bull was a character from a series of books by J. Arbuthnot in the 18th century. The books described him as an honest, goodhearted man representing Britain. As he became popular, political cartoonists began drawing him in their work. He was usually drawn as a fat man with a bulldog next to him. He also wore a suit, a top hat, and a waistcoat that looked like the *Union Jack. He often appeared in books, plays, and even as a brand name! However, since the 1950s, he has been seen less often. Nevertheless, British people still have a great love for him!

* Union Jack: the national flag of the United Kingdom

1 What is the passage mainly about?

a. A world-famous cartoonist
b. The history of British politics
c. A greatly loved character in Britain
d. British fashion trends in the 18th century

2 Write T if the statement is true or F if it's false.

1) John Bull has been a symbol of Britain since the 18th century.
2) John Bull has become even more popular since the 1950s.

VOCABULARY REVIEW

A Write the correct word next to its definition.

recruit	phrase	stand for	logo	mark

1 to write or draw letters or symbols on something: _____

2 an official symbol of an organization or company: _____

3 a group of words expressing a particular meaning: _____

4 to find a new person to work for a company or organization: _____

B Find the word that has a similar meaning to the underlined word.

1 Rachel grew up to resemble her mother in many ways.

   a. give up   *b.* think of   *c.* look like   *d.* worry about

2 Whenever I wear these pink shorts, people stare at me.

   a. laugh   *b.* look   *c.* shout   *d.* smile

C Choose the best word to complete each sentence.

1 All his friends call James by his _____, "Monkey."

   a. culture   *b.* barrel   *c.* cartoon   *d.* nickname

2 It's rude to _____ at people with your finger.

   a. draw   *b.* point   *c.* prepare   *d.* appear

3 The presidential election is the most important _____ event of the year.

   a. modern   *b.* successful   *c.* political   *d.* classical

4 There is no doubt that Michael Jackson was a pop music _____.

   a. viewer   *b.* icon   *c.* document   *d.* imagination

Differences in Shopping Behavior

"A man will pay \$2 for a \$1 item he needs. A woman will pay \$1 for a \$2 item she doesn't need." This is a joke that's true to reality. When it comes to shopping, <u>men</u>

5 <u>and women are from different planets.</u>

(①) Think about how men and women shop for jeans at the mall. (②) Men usually walk directly to the jeans store and buy them right away, without

10 searching for the best price. (③) They check out the discounts on a variety of other items they don't need, and they stop to do other things, such as test perfumes. (④)

So why do men and women shop so differently? Some scholars think

15 this is because of the difference in how men and women think. Men usually think of shopping as a mission to complete, so they try to do it quickly. On the contrary, women find it recreational and like taking their time to shop around.

Of course, this difference is not a matter of right and wrong. However, knowing these different ways of thinking can help men and women have fun together at the mall.

_____(A)_____, many department stores now have a men's lounge, where men can watch sports while their wives are shopping.

1 What is the best title for the passage?

   a. Be a Smart Shopper!

   b. Hot Places for Shopping

   c. Shopping Patterns by Gender

   d. Jeans: A Must-Have Item for Women

2 What does the underlined part mean?

   a. Men and women hate each other.

   b. Men and women are much the same.

   c. Men and women have little in common.

   d. Men and women should live apart from each other.

3 Where would the following sentence best fit?

> However, women usually buy jeans after wandering around the mall first.

   a. ①   *b.* ②   *c.* ③   *d.* ④

4 According to some scholars, men and women shop differently because
_____.

   a. they are interested in different items

   b. they have different ideas about shopping

   c. men think time is important but women don't

   d. women care more about saving money than men do

5 What is the best choice for blank (A)?

   a. As a result   *b.* In addition

   c. For example   *d.* In other words

6 Write T if the statement is true or F if it's false.

   1) Women tend to buy what they need quickly when shopping.

   2) Many department stores recently created special places for men.

Fill in the blanks with the correct words.

Shopping Patterns by Gender

How people shop for jeans
- Men: _____ go to one store and buy a pair of jeans
- Women: walk around the mall before buying jeans

A reason for the difference
- Men think of shopping as a _____, while women find it an enjoyable _____.

Understanding the difference
- Helps men and women have _____ together at the mall

fun	mission	pastime	quickly	discount

★ EXPANDING KNOWLEDGE ★

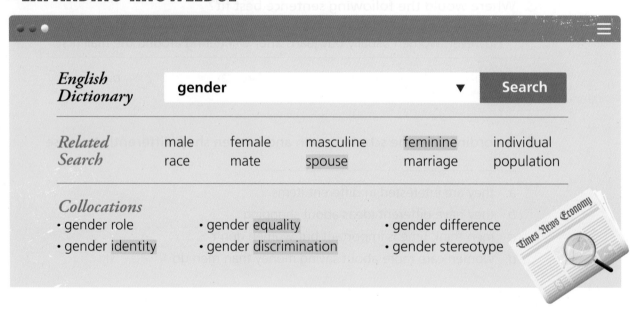

| English Dictionary | gender ▼ | | | | Search |

Related Search	male	female	masculine	feminine	individual
	race	mate	spouse	marriage	population

Collocations
- gender role
- gender identity
- gender equality
- gender discrimination
- gender difference
- gender stereotype

Write the correct highlighted word next to its definition.

1 one's wife or husband: _____

2 having qualities associated with women: _____

3 a situation in which people have the same rights: _____

4 unfair treatment of someone based on religion, race, etc.: _____

VOCABULARY REVIEW

A Write the correct word next to its definition.

lounge	scholar	item	recreational	mission

1 an important job that someone is given to do: _____

2 someone who studies a particular subject in detail: _____

3 a public room where many people can relax or wait: _____

4 related to activities that people do for enjoyment or pleasure: _____

B Find the word that has a similar meaning to the underlined word.

1 The project will be <u>completed</u> by the end of this year.

　　a. expected　　　*b.* finished　　　*c.* canceled　　　*d.* begun

2 They have <u>searched</u> for their lost cat for two days.

　　a. paid　　　*b.* cared　　　*c.* called　　　*d.* looked

C Choose the best word to complete each sentence.

1 This is the bus that goes _____ to Cherry Department Store.

　　a. tightly　　　*b.* highly　　　*c.* directly　　　*d.* partly

2 The little boy was _____ around the park when the police found him.

　　a. following　　　*b.* reading　　　*c.* working　　　*d.* wandering

3 The _____ of the room includes tax and a service charge.

　　a. offer　　　*b.* price　　　*c.* discount　　　*d.* shopping

4 He wanted to know the smallest _____ in our solar system.

　　a. thunder　　　*b.* variety　　　*c.* stage　　　*d.* planet

William Tell

A long time ago, Switzerland was ruled by a cruel man named Gessler. One day, he placed his hat on top of a tall pole and ordered the people to bow to it. But ...

A man named William Tell refused to bow.
5 Gessler became very angry and thought of a cruel plan to punish him. Gessler knew William Tell was a hunter and was very good at using a crossbow. So he ordered his soldiers to make
10 Tell's young son stand with an apple on his head. Then he ordered William Tell to shoot the apple with an arrow. Gessler told him, "If you don't, my soldiers will kill
15 your son."

William Tell was hesitant to do it. He asked, "What if my son should move? What if the arrow should miss the apple?" Then he begged, "Please! Don't make me do this." But Gessler ignored him. William
20 Tell's son, however, was not afraid. He had faith that his father was skilled enough to easily shoot the apple off his head. Quietly, William Tell picked up his crossbow and two arrows and took careful aim.

Whiz — (①) His arrow flew through the air and
25 struck the center of the apple, knocking it off his son's head! (②) The townspeople who had gathered around cheered with joy! (③) "Why did you pick up two arrows?" he asked William Tell. (④) Tell calmly replied, "If my child had been harmed, I would have shot the
30 second one through your heart."

1 **What is the best title for the passage?**

  a. Gessler and His Soldiers

  b. The Bravery of William Tell

  c. William Tell's Faith in Gessler

  d. The Magic Apple on a Boy's Head

2 **What does a cruel plan mean?**

  a. To steal William Tell's arrow

  b. To arrest William Tell and his son

  c. To have his soldiers kill William Tell's son

  d. To order William Tell to shoot an apple off his son's head

3 **What can be inferred from the underlined part in the 2nd paragraph?**

  a. William Tell didn't trust his son.

  b. William Tell didn't want to bow to the hat.

  c. William Tell was afraid he would hurt his son.

  d. William Tell was worried about losing his fame as a great hunter.

4 **Where would the following sentence best fit?**

Gessler grew angry, and then he saw the other arrow.

  a. ①   *b.* ②   *c.* ③   *d.* ④

5 **Which of the following does NOT describe Gessler?**

  a. evil   *b.* moral

  c. wicked   *d.* mean

6 **What is NOT true according to the passage?**

  a. Gessler was upset because William Tell didn't bow to his hat.

  b. Tell's son trusted that his father would be able to shoot the apple.

  c. People living in the town were pleased to see the arrow hit the apple.

  d. Tell intended to kill Gessler's soldiers with the other arrow.

Fill in the blanks with the correct words.

William Tell was a man who _____ to follow an order given by a cruel ruler named Gessler. This refusal made Gessler so angry that he decided to _____ him. He ordered Tell to shoot an apple off his son's head with an arrow. Even though Tell was a skilled hunter, he _____ because he was scared of hurting his son. Luckily, he _____ in shooting the apple. However, he had a second arrow to shoot at Gessler if his son had been harmed.

| hesitated | missed | refused | succeeded | punish |

★ EXPANDING KNOWLEDGE ★

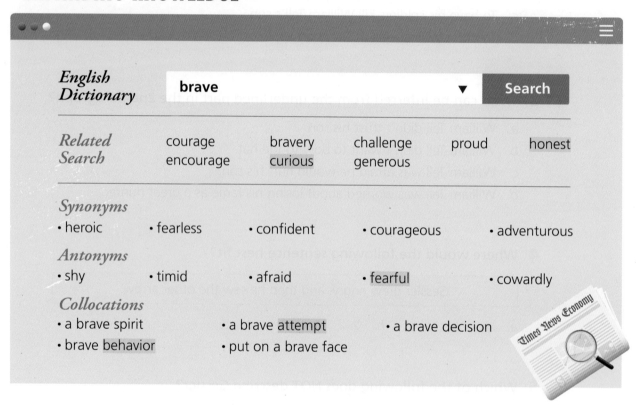

English Dictionary: brave ▼ | **Search**

Related Search: courage bravery challenge proud honest
encourage curious generous

Synonyms
- heroic
- fearless
- confident
- courageous
- adventurous

Antonyms
- shy
- timid
- afraid
- fearful
- cowardly

Collocations
- a brave spirit
- a brave attempt
- a brave decision
- brave behavior
- put on a brave face

Write the correct highlighted word next to its definition.

1 the way a person or animal acts: _____

2 an effort or try to do something: _____

3 wanting to learn more about something: _____

4 always telling the truth and not cheating: _____

VOCABULARY REVIEW

A Write the correct word next to its definition.

| rule | timid | heroic | beg | ignore |

1 to control a country: _____

2 without much courage or confidence: _____

3 to refuse to listen to or pay attention to: _____

4 to ask for something in a humble and urgent way: _____

B Find the word that has a similar meaning to the underlined word.

1 The team trained so hard that they are <u>confident</u> of winning the game.

   a. pleasant   *b.* certain   *c.* doubtful   *d.* shy

2 Dave kept lying, so Jenny has lost her <u>faith</u> in him.

   a. care   *b.* love   *c.* trust   *d.* curiosity

C Choose the best word to complete each sentence.

1 Jessica is _____ to marry Samuel because she thinks she's too young.

   a. mental   *b.* rare   *c.* hesitant   *d.* experienced

2 He committed a serious crime. He should be _____ for what he did.

   a. collected   *b.* punished   *c.* canceled   *d.* included

3 We need more _____ workers to finish this important project.

   a. scared   *b.* disappointed   *c.* confused   *d.* skilled

4 The _____ boy dove off the bridge into the river.

   a. smooth   *b.* latest   *c.* fearless   *d.* colorful

Before Reading
Have you ever been jealous of a friend who is better than you?

Antonio Salieri

Do you know who taught the great composers Beethoven, Schubert, and Liszt? Their teacher was a brilliant composer whose name was Antonio Salieri.

5 He might not be familiar to you, but he was a famous musician in Europe during his lifetime. He was hired by the Austrian emperor when he was in his 20s. And he worked as the royal court's chief composer for 38 years. During that time, he wrote wonderful operas, church songs, and other classical music.

10 But if Salieri was so great, why isn't he famous today? ① It's because of a rumor related to Mozart. ② Salieri was very successful, but people thought Mozart had a musical genius that Salieri didn't have. ③ To succeed in music, effort is more important than genius.

15 ④ Because of this, many believed Salieri was jealous of Mozart. Thus, when Mozart died suddenly, the rumor was born that Salieri had given him poison.

Since then, people have focused more on this rumor than his musical works. _____(A)_____, operas, plays, and movies tell this story. They make people think Salieri was just a jealous, common composer who murdered Mozart.

However, as new studies have shown that Mozart died of natural causes, many people are becoming more interested in Salieri and his works. And there's even an annual festival in Italy to celebrate his music!

1 **What is the best title for the passage?**

    a. Salieri: A Jealous Murderer

    b. Understanding Salieri's Music

    c. The Lives of Great Composers

    d. The Truth and the Myth about Salieri

2 **Why does the writer mention the underlined sentence?**

    a. To emphasize how brilliant Salieri was

    b. To compare Salieri with other great composers

    c. To show that Salieri lived at the same time as the others

    d. To explain how Salieri was influenced by the great composers

3 **Which sentence is NOT needed in the passage?**

    a. ①   *b.* ②   *c.* ③   *d.* ④

4 **What is the best choice for blank (A)?**

    a. Instead   *b.* Moreover

    c. However   *d.* Nevertheless

5 **Operas, plays, and movies that deal with the rumor about Salieri make people think** _____ .

6 **What is NOT true according to the passage?**

    a. Schubert was taught by Salieri.

    b. Salieri worked for the Austrian emperor for almost 40 years.

    c. There is no doubt that Salieri poisoned Mozart.

    d. Salieri's music is becoming more popular nowadays.

Fill in the blanks with the correct words.

Antonio Salieri was a famous _____ composer who taught other famous composers, including Beethoven, Schubert, and Liszt. Although he was great, he's not very well known today. It may be because of a rumor that Salieri was so _____ of Mozart that he poisoned him. However, new research has shown that Mozart died _____. Now, people are becoming _____ in Salieri's music again.

> proud   jealous   classical   naturally   interested

★ EXPANDING KNOWLEDGE ★

Encyclopedia Contents: Classical Music

1. History
   1.1 Early period (500–1600)
     1.1.1 Medieval music
     1.1.2 Renaissance music
   1.2 Common practice period
     (1600–1910)
     1.2.1 Baroque music
     1.2.2 Classical period music
     1.2.3 Romantic era music
   1.3 Modern and contemporary (1890–)

2. The instruments
   2.1 String
     2.1.1 Violin, viola, cello, etc.
   2.2 Woodwind
     2.2.1 Flute, clarinet, oboe, etc.
   2.3 Brass
     2.3.1 Horn, trumpet, trombone, etc.
   2.4 Percussion
     2.4.1 Drums, xylophone, timpani, etc.

1 Write the correct highlighted word next to its definition.

1) belonging to the present time: _____

2) relating to the period of the Middle Ages: _____

3) musical instruments that you play by hitting: _____

2 Write T if the statement is true or F if it's false.

1) The baroque style of music began to be written around the 17th century.

2) The brass instruments include flutes, horns, and trumpets.

Unit ⋆ 06
VOCABULARY REVIEW

A Write the correct word next to its definition.

poison	chief	genius	emperor	composer

1 highest in position or rank: _____

2 someone who writes music: _____

3 a very high level of intelligence or skill: _____

4 a substance that causes illness or death: _____

B Find the word that has a similar meaning to the underlined word.

1 Einstein was a brilliant scientist.

    a. diligent   *b.* powerful   *c.* intelligent   *d.* responsible

2 This book is about a politician who was murdered by a terrorist.

    a. hit   *b.* killed   *c.* raised   *d.* captured

C Choose the best word to complete each sentence.

1 Most children are very _____ with the story of Cinderella.

    a. brave   *b.* useful   *c.* familiar   *d.* available

2 As he was poor, John was _____ of his friend's wealth.

    a. full   *b.* afraid   *c.* jealous   *d.* capable

3 Mike enjoys listening to both _____ and modern music.

    a. cruel   *b.* classical   *c.* guilty   *d.* necessary

4 I heard a(n) _____ that Lisa is getting married next month.

    a. rumor   *b.* noise   *c.* scream   *d.* award

Doctors' Green Gowns

Q: Doctors usually wear white coats. So why do they always wear green gowns when performing surgery?

A: The color of the gowns worn in surgery was carefully chosen for several reasons. Most importantly, the color green helps
5   your eyes relax. After staring at bright red blood for a long time, doctors' eyes can get tired. But looking at the green color of their gown during surgery makes their eyes feel better.

Another reason is related to "afterimages." If people stare at one color for too long, it causes certain cells in their eyes to become tired.
10   Then, when they look at a white background, they see an afterimage — a floating shape of the opposite color. So when doctors wore white gowns, they saw afterimages that were green, the opposite color of red, on their gowns. ① However, this problem was easily solved by wearing green gowns. ② But some doctors still like wearing white gowns instead of green ones. ③ This is because the green color of the gowns prevents the afterimage of red blood. ④ As a result, doctors can concentrate on the surgery better.

_____(A)_____, wearing green during surgery helps to hide blood stains. Red blood stands out on white clothes. But on green clothes, the blood turns brown, and you hardly even notice it.

So there are three good reasons why doctors wear green gowns!

1 What is the passage mainly about?

    a. Ways to keep white coats clean

    b. Different kinds of doctors' gowns

    c. How to prevent your eyes from getting tired

    d. The advantages of doctors wearing green gowns

2 What makes doctors' eyes feel better during surgery?

_____

3 Match the sequence of how an afterimage is made in order from (A) to (C).

You stare at one color. → _____ (A) _____ → _____ (B) _____ → _____ (C) _____

    1) (A) •   • *a.* An afterimage appears.

    2) (B) •   • *b.* You look at a white background.

    3) (C) •   • *c.* Some cells in your eyes become tired.

4 Which sentence is NOT needed in the passage?

    a. ①   *b.* ②   *c.* ③   *d.* ④

5 Which is the best choice for blank (A)?

    a. However   *b.* Therefore

    c. In addition   *d.* For example

6 What is NOT mentioned in the passage?

    a. Why the color green is good for the eyes

    b. Which color is the opposite of red

    c. Why doctors in surgery began wearing green gowns

    d. How to clean blood stains from clothes

Fill in the blanks with the correct words.

Why Doctors Wear Green Gowns during Surgery

1 The color green _____ a doctor's eyes.

2 They _____ afterimages.
• Staring at red blood makes green afterimages.
• Looking at a green background stops afterimages.

3 They _____ red stains.
• Blood is less _____ on green gowns than on white ones.

> prevent   relaxes   noticeable   cells   hide

★ EXPANDING KNOWLEDGE ★

English Dictionary

| vision | ▼ | Search |

| Related Search | view | sense | sight | image | visible |
| | visual | inspire | mission | illusion | |

Noun

1. [uncountable] the ability to see (= sight)
   He suffered loss of vision after the car accident.

2. [countable] an idea of what you think something should be like
   He had a clear vision of how he would make his dream come true.

Collocations from the 1st sense

• night vision   • normal vision   • poor vision   • 20-20 vision

Times News Economy

Write the correct highlighted word next to its definition.

1 something that is not what it seems to be: _____

2 related to an ordinary type, level, or pattern: _____

3 to give someone the confidence to do something well: _____

4 one of the five abilities you have to see, hear, smell, taste, and feel things: _____

VOCABULARY REVIEW

A Write the correct word next to its definition.

perform	relax	afterimage	cell	shape

1 to do work, a duty, or a task: _____

2 to feel calm and comfortable: _____

3 the smallest part of a living thing: _____

4 the image that you continue to see after the original image is gone: _____

B Find the word that has a similar meaning to the underlined word.

1 To prevent injuries you should always stretch before exercising.

    a. cure   *b.* cause   *c.* avoid   *d.* decrease

2 Fortunately, the surgery was effective, and the patient is getting better.

    a. operation   *b.* recovery   *c.* background   *d.* disease

C Choose the best word to complete each sentence.

1 They said goodbye to each other and walked off in _____ directions.

    a. strict   *b.* secret   *c.* simple   *d.* opposite

2 I can't _____ on my homework with all that noise.

    a. rely   *b.* put   *c.* concentrate   *d.* decide

3 I spilled ink on my sweater, and it left a(n) _____.

    a. drawing   *b.* stain   *c.* image   *d.* design

4 The ads _____ and catch people's attention.

    a. stand by   *b.* stand out   *c.* stand up   *d.* stand aside

Coffeehouses: More than Drinking Coffee

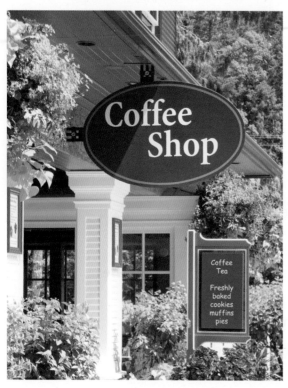

These days, coffee shops can be found everywhere. However, their popularity is nothing new. In 17th and 18th-century England, coffee shops were just as popular as they are today.

Coffee was first introduced to England in the 16th century. Before coffee was brought to England, people mostly drank beer and wine. However, coffee soon became popular because people considered it to be a healthy drink. They thought it inspired creativity and provided energy. ① In 1650, the first English coffeehouse opened in Oxford. ② But in other regions, coffeehouses were unpopular. ③ Soon coffeehouses began to spread throughout the country. ④ After only 25 years, there were more than 3,000 coffeehouses across England.

The popularity of coffee was not the only reason for the spread of coffeehouses. At that time, coffeehouses were popular

20 _____(A)_____. People went to coffeehouses to drink coffee, learn the news of the day, or meet people from various backgrounds. They also discussed a variety of topics ranging from politics and philosophy to science and business. Moreover, for just one penny, people could not only buy a cup of coffee but

25 also borrow a newspaper or a book to read.
_____(B)_____, these coffeehouses were called "penny universities."

All of this made coffeehouses the main intellectual centers during the 17th and

30 18th centuries in England.

1 **What is the passage mainly about?**

   a. The importance of education

   b. The benefits of drinking coffee

   c. Various kinds of English coffeehouses

   d. The long-lasting popularity of English coffeehouses

2 **Why did people in England think of coffee as a healthy drink?**

_____

3 **Which sentence is NOT needed in the passage?**

   a. ①   *b.* ②   *c.* ③   *d.* ④

4 **What is the best choice for blank (A)?**

   a. places for youth

   b. tourist attractions

   c. science institutions

   d. places for social interaction

5 **What is the best choice for blank (B)?**

   a. However   *b.* In addition

   c. As a result   *d.* In other words

6 **What is NOT mentioned in the passage?**

   a. When the first English coffeehouse opened

   b. Why the first English coffeehouse opened in Oxford

   c. What people did in coffeehouses

   d. How much money people had to pay for a cup of coffee

Fill in the blanks with the correct words.

In 17th and 18th-century England, coffee became very _____ because people thought it was _____. The first coffeehouse was opened in Oxford in 1650, and in a few years there were lots of coffeehouses all over the country. People didn't just drink coffee there. They went there to meet people and _____ various intellectual topics. People could even borrow a newspaper or a book to read when they bought a one-penny cup of coffee. That's why people began calling coffeehouses "penny _____."

discuss	healthy	popular	provide	universities

★ EXPANDING KNOWLEDGE ★

Encyclopedia Contents: Coffee

1. History
2. Cultivation
   2.1 Top five coffee producers in order: Brazil, Vietnam, Indonesia, Colombia, Ethiopia
3. Process
   3.1 Roasting
   3.2 Grinding
   3.3 Brewing
4. Health benefits
   4.1 Improvement in energy level
   4.2 Rich in antioxidants
5. Health risks
   5.1 Cause of high blood pressure
   5.2 Dehydration
6. Social issue
   6.1 Fair trade

1 Write the correct highlighted word next to its definition.

1) having a lot of something: _____

2) relating to human society: _____

3) the process of raising crops and plants: _____

2 Write T if the statement is true or F if it's false.

1) Brazil produces more coffee than any other country in the world.

2) Coffee is a recommended drink for those with high blood pressure.

VOCABULARY REVIEW

A Write the correct word next to its definition.

unpopular	spread	philosophy	topic	variety

1 not liked by most people: _____

2 to grow in number and popularity: _____

3 a subject people talk or write about: _____

4 the study of life and the meaning of existence: _____

B Find the word that has a similar meaning to the underlined word.

1 This book <u>provides</u> information on more than 1,000 birds.

   a. confirms   *b.* gives   *c.* takes   *d.* proves

2 Buddhism was first <u>introduced</u> into China from India during the Han dynasty.

   a. brought   *b.* started   *c.* stolen   *d.* spoken

C Choose the best word to complete each sentence.

1 A good teacher _____ a love of learning in students.

   a. inspires   *b.* changes   *c.* discourages   *d.* weakens

2 The population of these cities _____ between 3 and 5 million.

   a. joins   *b.* goes   *c.* ranges   *d.* becomes

3 Serena reads many books and newspapers for her _____ development.

   a. emotional   *b.* spiritual   *c.* intellectual   *d.* physical

4 China shares a similar cultural _____ with Korea.

   a. field   *b.* category   *c.* rank   *d.* background

Before Reading
Do you know of any festivals held in India?

The Holi Festival in India

People are throwing red powder at each other. Some are even throwing balloons filled with yellow water at strangers. Children with water pistols are also spraying each other. But surprisingly, no one gets angry. Rather, everyone looks happy. What is happening? These people are celebrating
5 Holi, one of the most exciting festivals in India!

Holi is celebrated on the day after the full moon in March every year. It is held to welcome spring and to pray for a good harvest. During the festival, people decorate themselves with colorful powders made from flowers and vegetables. Each color has a unique meaning. _____(A)_____, red
10 represents energy and green means harmony.

Holi is also related to the story of Holika, the sister of King Hiranyakasipu. The king believed he was greater than the gods. So when his son Prahlad worshipped a god instead of him, the king got angry and told Holika to kill Prahlad. This wicked woman tried to kill her young nephew in
15 a fire, but her plan went wrong. In the end, she burned to death instead of Prahlad. To celebrate <u>this</u>, people light huge bonfires the night before the festival.

Today, not only Indians but also visitors from around the world enjoy Holi. People at the festival end up covered in various colors, which unites everyone as if they were one big color palette!

1 What is the best title for the passage?

　　a. The Worst Festival in India

　　b. Holi: The Festival of Colors

　　c. The Death of Wicked Holika

　　d. The Danger of the Holi Festival

2 Which of the following best describes the mood of the 1st paragraph?

　　a. lively

　　b. boring

　　c. gloomy

　　d. frightening

3 What is the best choice for blank (A)?

　　a. Besides

　　b. Similarly

　　c. Therefore

　　d. For example

4 Why did King Hiranyakasipu tell his sister Holika to kill his son?

_____

5 What does the underlined part refer to?

　　a. Holika burning to death

　　b. Prahlad not obeying his father

　　c. Holika trying to kill her nephew

　　d. The king thinking he was greater than the gods

6 What is NOT true according to the passage?

　　a. People throw colored powder at each other during the Holi Festival.

　　b. Holi is held on the day after the full moon every March.

　　c. Only powders made from chemicals are used during the festival.

　　d. Both Indians and foreigners participate in Holi together.

Fill in the blanks with the correct words.

The Holi Festival

- Celebrated by throwing _____ powder and spraying water at people
- Held on the day after the full moon in _____ every year
- Related to a legend: Holika, a(n) _____ woman, tried to kill her nephew but failed and died.
- _____ by both Indians and tourists from around the world

March   colored   enjoyed   wicked   decorated

★ EXPANDING KNOWLEDGE ★

Encyclopedia Contents: Festivals

1. Purposes
 1.1 Cultural events
 1.2 Celebrations
 1.3 Entertainment
2. Features
 2.1 Parades, fireworks, etc.
 2.2 Special foods and beverages
 2.3 Music and dancing
 2.4 Costumes

3. Types
 3.1 Religious festivals
 3.2 Arts festivals: film, literature, etc.
  3.2.1 Cannes Film Festival (France)
 3.3 Food and drink festivals
  3.3.1 La Tomatina (tomato, Spain)
  3.3.2 Oktoberfest (beer, Germany)
 3.4 Seasonal festivals
  3.4.1 Halloween (America)

1 Write the correct highlighted word next to its definition.

 1) related to believing in and worshipping a god: _____

 2) the act of giving performances that people enjoy: _____

 3) pieces of writing that are considered works of art: _____

2 Write T if the statement is true or F if it's false.

 1) Festivals usually feature entertaining activities.

 2) Oktoberfest is a festival that has a background in art.

VOCABULARY REVIEW

A Write the correct word next to its definition.

pistol	stranger	unite	worship	represent

1 someone you do not know: _____

2 to join people or things together: _____

3 a small gun you can hold in one hand: _____

4 to show respect and affection for a god: _____

B Find the word that has a similar meaning to the underlined word.

1 I can't believe the little boys did such wicked things.

　a. bad　　　　*b.* great　　　　*c.* creative　　　　*d.* unexpected

2 His health problems are directly related to smoking.

　a. similar　　　*b.* confused　　　*c.* connected　　　*d.* annoyed

C Choose the best word to complete each sentence.

1 This year's Christmas tree was beautifully _____.

　a. pressed　　　*b.* sprayed　　　*c.* decreased　　　*d.* decorated

2 Next, mix curry _____ with five glasses of water.

　a. festival　　　*b.* recipe　　　*c.* powder　　　*d.* standard

3 Many people in the small village _____ the medical team.

　a. welcomed　　*b.* planted　　　*c.* considered　　*d.* published

4 The _____ display attracted lots of people from all over the country.

　a. conditions　　*b.* fireworks　　*c.* affection　　　*d.* emotions

The Orsay Museum

The Orsay Museum is one of the most famous attractions in Paris. ① It is located on the left bank of the Seine River across from the Louvre Museum. ② The museum holds many priceless works of art, including paintings by Renoir, Monet, and Van Gogh. ③ Unfortunately, Van Gogh killed himself with a gun. ④ Almost all of the art in the museum was created in France between 1848 and 1914, during the Impressionist period. So, the Orsay is the largest Impressionist museum in the world.

Surprisingly, the building wasn't a museum at first. In fact, it was built to be a train station! For almost 40 years, it was a part of the railroad network. However, it was eventually abandoned because modern, longer trains didn't fit on its short platforms.

In 1986, it reopened as a museum to house a huge collection of paintings, sculptures, and photography. Not only is the art inside the museum amazing, but the museum building itself is a work of art. Since it was converted from a train station, the building has some distinctive features. _____(A)_____, it has a high, elegant, domed ceiling made of glass, which lets lots of sunlight in. This allows visitors to view the artwork better. It also features a huge, round clock near its entrance. Today, more than three million people visit the museum every year.

1 What is the best title for the passage?

   a. France: The Treasure Chest of Modern Art

   b. The Modern Design of the Orsay Museum

   c. The Great Works of Famous Impressionists

   d. From Train Station to Impressionist Museum

2 Which sentence is NOT needed in the passage?

   a. ①   *b.* ②   *c.* ③   *d.* ④

3 Why was the Orsay building removed from the railroad network?

_____

4 What does the underlined sentence mean?

   a. The museum was originally built as a work of art.

   b. The museum building is much more beautiful than the artwork inside.

   c. The artwork in the museum is amazing, but the building itself is very old.

   d. As well as housing an amazing collection of art, the museum building itself is beautiful.

5 What is the best choice for the blank (A)?

   a. Similarly   *b.* In addition

   c. For example   *d.* On the other hand

6 Write T if the statement is true or F if it's false.

   1) Lots of sunlight inside the museum makes it hard to view the art.

   2) The Orsay Museum's building still shows some of its former train station features.

STRATEGIC ORGANIZER

Fill in the blanks with the correct words.

The Orsay Museum

• Located on the left _____ of the Seine River
• Holds a lot of _____ art
• Originally built as a(n) _____
• Reopened as a museum in 1986
• Features a high, elegant, domed _____ made of glass and a big round clock

bank   ceiling   visitors   train station   Impressionist

★ EXPANDING KNOWLEDGE ★

Encyclopedia Contents: Art (Paintings)

1. Types of art
  1.1 Portrait
  1.2 Landscape
  1.3 Still life
2. Styles of art and artists
  2.1 Impressionism: Monet, Renoir, Van Gogh
  2.2 Expressionism: Munch
  2.3 Cubism: Picasso, Braque
  2.4 Realism: Degas

3. Famous art museums in the world
  3.1 The Metropolitan Museum of Art (New York, America)
  3.2 The British Museum (London, England)
  3.3 The Louvre Museum (Paris, France)
  3.4 The State Hermitage Museum (Saint Petersburg, Russia)

1 Write the correct highlighted word next to its definition.

1) a painting or photograph of someone: _____

2) a picture showing an area of countryside: _____

3) a style of art which shows someone or something as it is in real life: _____

2 Write T if the statement is true or F if it's false.

1) Renoir and Picasso are famous Impressionists.

2) The Metropolitan Museum of Art is located in New York.

Unit ★ 10
VOCABULARY REVIEW

A Write the correct word next to its definition.

create	distinctive	abandon	elegant	period

1 to leave something forever: _____

2 clearly different from others: _____

3 to make or invent something: _____

4 a length of time with a beginning and an end: _____

B Find the word that has a similar meaning to the underlined word.

1 From the terrace, you can <u>view</u> the beautiful garden and pond.

    a. call   *b.* see   *c.* find   *d.* make

2 The police arrested the woman who had stolen the <u>priceless</u> paintings.

    a. cheap   *b.* modern   *c.* graceful   *d.* valuable

C Choose the best word to complete each sentence.

1 Plants can't grow well if they don't get enough _____.

    a. weeds   *b.* worms   *c.* sunlight   *d.* features

2 I'm thinking about _____ the spare room into an office.

    a. renting   *b.* converting   *c.* sharing   *d.* moving

3 This museum is a famous _____ visited by millions of people every year.

    a. ceiling   *b.* attraction   *c.* collection   *d.* railroad

4 The ice _____ was made to celebrate the 10th anniversary of the company.

    a. agriculture   *b.* individual   *c.* expression   *d.* sculpture

ENTERTAINMENT

Video Games Live

Video Games Live is a world-touring concert where music from popular video games is played. When Video Games Live came to L.A., I couldn't miss it. The orchestra performed music from my favorite video games. At the same time, scenes from the games appeared on

5 a giant screen, making the concert very dramatic!

   Some of the songs came from old games like *Pong* and *Space Invaders*. Before the concert, I couldn't imagine how the orchestra would play them, because they use only short, simple sounds over and over. But they cleverly used instruments like drums and cymbals to produce the "bleep-bloop"

10 and "dun-dun-dun" sounds of these games. Songs from newer games like *StarCraft* and *Final Fantasy* were also performed. They were much grander and more complicated than the old game music. When the orchestra played them, it was more like a real classical music concert.

   But my favorite part was a performance by Martin Leung,

15 the video game pianist. ① He played a medley of game songs beautifully. ② I was amazed when he played a song from *Super Mario World* at about twice its original speed. ③ It is not too much to say that speed of music is

20 very important when playing a game. ④ People cheered the loudest for him.

   Besides the music, there were also many other entertaining things. It was fun to see people dressed up as game characters for the costume contest. And the laser show was amazing! I was glad to see people of all ages enjoying this event together.

1 What is the passage mainly about?

    a. A unique type of concert

    b. A brand-new video game

    c. Various types of orchestras

    d. World-famous video games

2 Why couldn't the writer imagine how the songs from classic video games would be played?

_____

3 Which sentence is NOT needed in the passage?

    a. ①   *b.* ②   *c.* ③   *d.* ④

4 Who is NOT talking about their experience at Video Games Live?

    a. Victoria: I dressed like the princess from *Super Mario World*.

    b. Eric: The sounds from the games made playing them more exciting.

    c. Kay: It was wonderful to see the pianist's hands move amazingly fast.

    d. Crystal: It was fun to hear the repetitive sounds of drums and cymbals.

5 What is NOT mentioned about Video Games Live?

    a. Where the music the orchestra played was from

    b. How the orchestra expressed the sounds of the game music

    c. How many songs were played during the concert

    d. Which performance the writer liked the best

6 Write T if the statement is true or F if it's false.

    1) Images from video games were shown on a screen during the concert.

    2) Classical music was played instead of modern game music.

STRATEGIC SUMMARY

Fill in the blanks with the correct words.

Video Games Live is a unique concert where a(n) _____ plays video game music. They perform songs from old games as well as newer ones. When they play old songs, they cleverly use musical instruments to make short, _____ sounds from those games. Songs from newer games are more like _____ music. The concert also features Martin Leung, a video game pianist who can play game music very fast. Besides music, Video Games Live has other attractions, such as a(n) _____ contest and laser show. People of all ages come and enjoy the event.

quiet	orchestra	costume	simple	classical

★ EXPANDING KNOWLEDGE ★

English Dictionary

entertaining ▼   **Search**

Related Search

amusement performance	exhibition crowd	broadcast audience	impression

Synonyms
• amusing   • pleasing   • enjoyable   • delightful   • fascinating

Antonyms
• boring   • depressing   • dull   • uninteresting

Collocations
• an entertaining hour   • an entertaining topic   • an entertaining speech

Write the correct highlighted word next to its definition.

1 the people who watch or listen to a performance: _____

2 an idea or feeling you get about someone or something: _____

3 to send out messages or programs on television or radio: _____

4 a show of artwork or other objects that you can go to see: _____

Unit★11
VOCABULARY REVIEW

A Write the correct word next to its definition.

character	medley	giant	orchestra	dramatic

1 extremely large: _____

2 exciting or impressive: _____

3 a person in a film, book, or game: _____

4 a large group of people playing various instruments together: _____

B Find the word that has a similar meaning to the underlined word.

1 Doctors were <u>amazed</u> at her rapid recovery.

   a. angry   *b.* surprised   *c.* happy   *d.* grateful

2 The process of making this bread isn't <u>complicated</u>.

   a. complex   *b.* creative   *c.* quiet   *d.* real

C Choose the best word to complete each sentence.

1 The city offers a variety of _____ and attractions you can enjoy.

   a. genres   *b.* fields   *c.* reservations   *d.* amusements

2 My brother was _____ as a ghost for Halloween.

   a. looked up   *b.* taken up   *c.* dressed up   *d.* caught up

3 I greatly enjoyed this documentary. It was absolutely _____.

   a. boring   *b.* fascinating   *c.* disappointing   *d.* responsible

4 He gave me a copy of the _____ document.

   a. smart   *b.* possible   *c.* original   *d.* confident

Before Reading
Do you know any species that have gone extinct because of human beings?

Dodo Birds

The expression "as dead as a dodo" means "completely dead." Dodo birds once lived on the African island of Mauritius. However, as the phrase suggests, the species disappeared over 300 years ago.

Before the dodo became extinct, its home, Mauritius, was a paradise

5 for the bird. It was isolated from the rest of the world, and there were no enemies to fear. Also, seeds and fruit, the bird's main food, were easily found on the ground. Thanks to its environment, the dodo didn't need to fly, so it gradually evolved into a ground-bound bird like the chicken. Its wings became small, while its body size increased. The dodo was about a

10 meter high and weighed up to 23 kg.

Around 1600, Spanish and Portuguese explorers first saw the bird. They named it the dodo, based on the Portuguese word for "fool." They thought the bird was foolish because it wasn't afraid of people or other animals. Unfortunately, this made it

15 _____(A)_____. Animals like

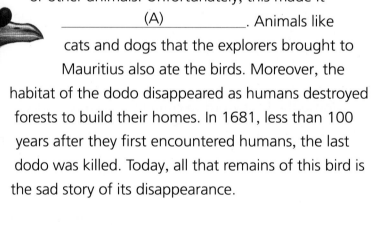

cats and dogs that the explorers brought to Mauritius also ate the birds. Moreover, the habitat of the dodo disappeared as humans destroyed forests to build their homes. In 1681, less than 100 years after they first encountered humans, the last dodo was killed. Today, all that remains of this bird is the sad story of its disappearance.

1 **What is the best title for the passage?**

    a. The Sad Fate of the Dodo

    b. The Dodo Needs Our Help!

    c. The Dodo: An Imaginary Animal

    d. The Dodo: A Newly Found Species

2 **Why does the writer mention <u>a paradise</u>?**

    a. To describe the beauty of the island

    b. To explain that the island was the same as others

    c. To show how comfortable the island was for the dodo

    d. To give an example of a place where people want to visit

3 **What is the main point of the 2nd paragraph?**

    a. The island was the only place where the dodo had lived.

    b. There was a lot of food for the dodo to eat on the island.

    c. The dodo's small wings were convenient for living on the island.

    d. The dodo had changed according to the environment of the island.

4 **Why did Spanish and Portuguese explorers think the dodo was foolish?**

    _____

5 **What is the best choice for blank (A)?**

    a. stay away from people

    b. popular among explorers

    c. a true friend to other animals

    d. an easy target for hungry hunters

6 **What is NOT mentioned about the dodo?**

    a. Where it lived

    b. When it became extinct

    c. How big it was

    d. How it tasted

Fill in the blanks with the correct words.

The dodo is a bird species that became _____ over 300 years ago. It used to live on the African island of Mauritius, which was the perfect place for the bird. Since it could easily find food on the ground, the dodo _____ into a huge ground-bound bird. It thrived on the island until European _____ arrived there around 1600. Humans hunted the dodos and _____ their habitat. This caused the dodo to disappear within 100 years of humans' arrival on the island.

| explorers | extinct | evolved | disappear | destroyed |

★ EXPANDING KNOWLEDGE ★

Sadly, not only is the dodo bird extinct, but a tree on Mauritius is in danger of meeting the same fate. It is called the dodo tree. Scientists found that no new dodo trees have grown on the island since the dodo bird went extinct. They believe the bird helped the tree's seeds grow. Dodos bit through the seeds' tough shells when they ate them. The seeds later exited the dodos' bodies through their droppings and were able to grow. Without the dodo bird, new trees haven't been able to grow! Fortunately, however, scientists found that turkeys can also help the seeds grow. So hopefully the dodo tree will not end up "as dead as a dodo."

1 **What is the passage mainly about?**

a. Why the dodo bird liked the dodo tree

b. How the dodo tree survives on Mauritius

c. Why the dodo tree has almost become extinct

d. How the weather in Mauritius has affected its ecosystem

2 **Write T if the statement is true or F if it's false.**

1) Scientists believe the dodo bird went extinct because it ate the dodo tree's seeds.

2) It is believed that turkeys may be able to prevent the dodo tree's extinction.

Unit 12
VOCABULARY REVIEW

A Write the correct word next to its definition.

| weigh | evolve | forest | explorer | encounter |

1 a large area of land covered with trees: _____

2 to meet someone or something unexpectedly: _____

3 to change physically over a long period of time: _____

4 someone who travels to places that aren't known to others: _____

B Find the word that has the opposite meaning of the underlined word.

1 Our aircraft was attacked by the <u>enemy</u>.

   a. stranger   *b.* traveler   *c.* relative   *d.* friend

2 With her parents' care, Sophia <u>gradually</u> recovered from her illness.

   a. slowly   *b.* regularly   *c.* suddenly   *d.* especially

C Choose the best word to complete each sentence.

1 You need to separate the food waste from the _____.

   a. end   *b.* rest   *c.* story   *d.* phrase

2 We'll plant various flower _____ in our garden tomorrow.

   a. seeds   *b.* vases   *c.* pots   *d.* fruits

3 The scientist discovered a new _____ of bird in a remote area.

   a. tool   *b.* species   *c.* ocean   *d.* muscle

4 The town was so _____ that it took several hours to reach it.

   a. suggested   *b.* extinct   *c.* isolated   *d.* developed

ARCHITECTURE

Before Reading
If you were going to choose a new home, what would you look for?

The Discomfort of Home

Homes give us great comfort. That's what they are for! But artists Shusaku Arakawa and Madeline Gins had a different and unique idea of home. So, they created the Reversible Destiny Lofts, apartments that can change people's lives, in Tokyo.

5   From the outside, these apartments look like Lego blocks, with spheres, tubes, and cubes. Moreover, each part is painted red, orange, pink, or blue, like an indoor playground in a fast food restaurant. The inside is even more surprising. The floors are not flat but bumpy like a chocolate chip cookie. The kitchen has a floor that drops down suddenly. Every light switch is in an

10 unexpected place, so you need to feel around to turn on the light. Plus, the door to the veranda is so small that you have to crawl like a baby to get out!

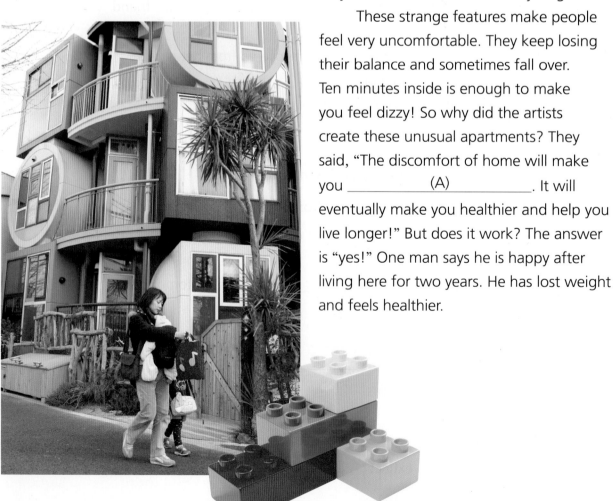

These strange features make people feel very uncomfortable. They keep losing their balance and sometimes fall over. Ten minutes inside is enough to make you feel dizzy! So why did the artists create these unusual apartments? They said, "The discomfort of home will make you _____(A)_____. It will eventually make you healthier and help you live longer!" But does it work? The answer is "yes!" One man says he is happy after living here for two years. He has lost weight and feels healthier.

1 What is the best title for the passage?

    a. A New Amusement Park in Tokyo

    b. How Safe Are Indoor Playgrounds?

    c. The Latest Housing Trends in Tokyo

    d. New Creative Homes for Healthy Living

2 What is NOT used to describe the features of the Reversible Destiny Lofts?

    a. Lego blocks

    b. a playground in a fast food restaurant

    c. a chocolate chip cookie

    d. a baby

3 Why do you need to feel around to turn on the light in the Reversible Destiny Lofts?

_____

4 What is the best choice for blank (A)?

    a. feel relaxed

    b. lazy and sleepy

    c. angry and upset

    d. become more active

5 Who is NOT talking about his or her life in the Reversible Destiny Lofts?

    a. Crystal: I like to lie on the floor and feel its smooth surface.

    b. Kay: I sometimes hit my head when I go out to the veranda.

    c. Jessica: I always have a hard time keeping my balance when walking.

    d. Nick: I try to be careful not to miss my step whenever I enter the kitchen.

6 Write T if the statement is true or F if it's false.

    1) There is a fast food restaurant in the apartment building.

    2) The Reversible Destiny Lofts were built to improve people's health.

Fill in the blanks with the correct words.

| The Reversible Destiny Lofts | Apartments designed to be _____ homes |

Features
- Outside: shaped like Lego blocks and painted in a variety of bright _____
- Inside: _____ floors, a deep kitchen floor, light switches that are hard to _____, and small veranda doors

Purpose • To help people live healthier and longer lives

| bumpy | flat | uncomfortable | find | colors |

★ EXPANDING KNOWLEDGE ★

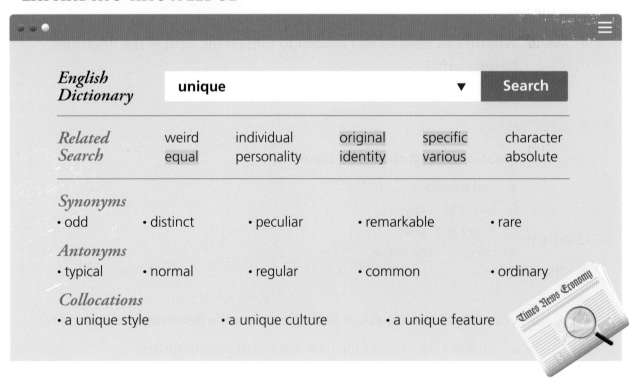

| English Dictionary | unique ▼ | Search |

| Related Search | weird | individual | original | specific | character |
| | equal | personality | identity | various | absolute |

Synonyms
- odd
- distinct
- peculiar
- remarkable
- rare

Antonyms
- typical
- normal
- regular
- common
- ordinary

Collocations
- a unique style
- a unique culture
- a unique feature

Write the correct highlighted word next to its definition.

1 of several different types: _____

2 existing first or at the beginning: _____

3 having the same quantity, size, or value: _____

4 qualities that make someone or something different: _____

VOCABULARY REVIEW

A Write the correct word next to its definition.

flat	crawl	bumpy	odd	destiny

1 not normal or expected: _____

2 the things that must happen in the future: _____

3 to move around on your hands and knees: _____

4 not smooth and having lots of raised areas: _____

B Find the word that has a similar meaning to the underlined word.

1 Wendy <u>eventually</u> agreed with the decision.

    a. never   *b.* easily   *c.* finally   *d.* surprisingly

2 He has had an <u>unusual</u> talent for languages since childhood.

    a. unwanted   *b.* hidden   *c.* real   *d.* uncommon

C Choose the best word to complete each sentence.

1 The silk we produce is much softer than _____ silk.

    a. correct   *b.* regular   *c.* confused   *d.* delicious

2 The best _____ of the resort is its large swimming pool.

    a. member   *b.* discomfort   *c.* feature   *d.* material

3 It made me _____ to look down from the high tower.

    a. dizzy   *b.* direct   *c.* normal   *d.* exact

4 This skirt is too small for me because I have gained a lot of _____.

    a. balance   *b.* spheres   *c.* knowledge   *d.* weight

The Living Library

These days, we can do lots of things in libraries. We can use the Internet, borrow music, or even take classes! But, did you know there's a library where you can borrow a person? It is called the Living Library!

The Living Library was founded in Denmark in 2000. Now there are
5 lots of Living Libraries around the world! What these libraries lend people are "living books" — people who are often _____(A)_____. Some examples might be bus drivers and feminists, who are often considered aggressive. Another example would be vegetarians, who are thought of as sensitive. When library users borrow a living book, they can talk to the person for 30
10 minutes.

So why was this unique library created? According to Ronni Abergel, the founder of the Living Library, we often have negative prejudices against certain people. If we just spend some time talking to them, we can learn who they really are and eventually break our prejudices!

15 At the Living Library, we can experience this. For example, people tend to think that pro gamers are addicted to games. But, if you actually spent time talking to a pro gamer, you might realize he is not addicted. Perhaps he only practices playing games a lot to be good at his job. In this way, the Living Library teaches us an important lesson: _____(B)_____

1 **What is the best title for the passage?**

   a. Tips for Using Public Libraries

   b. Various Features of Modern Libraries

   c. The Key to Making Good Conversation

   d. Meet a Human Book to Open Your Mind

2 **What is the best choice for blank (A)?**

   a. poor   *b.* active

   c. respected   *d.* misunderstood

3 **What can we do by talking to people we have negative prejudices against?**

_____

4 **Why does the writer mention pro gamers?**

   a. To show how exciting the libraries are

   b. To introduce a job that is popular with teenagers

   c. To explain why addiction to computer games is dangerous

   d. To give an example of people about whom we have negative ideas

5 **What is the best choice for blank (B)?**

   a. Easier said than done.

   b. Never judge a book by its cover.

   c. A friend in need is a friend indeed.

   d. When in Rome, do as the Romans do.

6 **Write T if the statement is true or F if it's false.**

   1) The Living Library is popular only in Denmark.

   2) Users can talk to the living books for half an hour.

STRATEGIC ORGANIZER

Fill in the blanks with the correct words.

The Living Library

What it is
- It is a library where people can _____ a person.
- It was founded in Denmark in 2000.

How it works
- People _____ to "living books" for 30 minutes.
- "Living books" are people who are usually _____.
- People can break their _____ by talking with "living books."

| talk | consist | borrow | prejudices | misunderstood |

★ EXPANDING KNOWLEDGE ★

English Dictionary

| viewpoint ▼ | Search |

| *Related Search* | objective
opinion | subjective
prejudice | optimistic
bias | pessimistic
attitude |

Synonyms
- view
- angle
- outlook
- perspective
- standpoint

Collocations
- a historical viewpoint
- a critical viewpoint
- a narrow viewpoint
- a different viewpoint
- a personal viewpoint

Write the correct highlighted word next to its definition.

1 hopeful about the future: _____

2 expecting the worst possible result: _____

3 based on personal opinions and beliefs: _____

4 expressing an opinion that something is wrong: _____

VOCABULARY REVIEW

A Write the correct word next to its definition.

realize	addicted	negative	library	lend

1 to start to know or understand something: _____

2 considering only the bad sides of something: _____

3 a place where you can look at or borrow books: _____

4 unable to stop doing something because you like it so much: _____

B Find the word that has a similar meaning to the underlined word.

1 Everyone wore a <u>unique</u> costume to the Halloween party.

    a. certain   *b.* general   *c.* unusual   *d.* common

2 The art school was <u>founded</u> in 1978.

    a. moved   *b.* located   *c.* stopped   *d.* established

C Choose the best word to complete each sentence.

1 She is so _____ about her weight that she hardly eats anything.

    a. natural   *b.* noisy   *c.* generous   *d.* sensitive

2 Lauren has _____ the piano hard for the contest next week.

    a. spent   *b.* enjoyed   *c.* practiced   *d.* completed

3 Many people still have a _____ against the disabled.

    a. process   *b.* feminist   *c.* founder   *d.* prejudice

4 I don't know why my brother shows _____ and violent behavior.

    a. calm   *b.* aggressive   *c.* separate   *d.* comfortable

Before Reading

When you go to an aquarium, what do you enjoy seeing the most?

Training Sea Mammals

Richard Maddox, a sea mammal trainer at Sea World, tells us about his job.

Q: What does a sea mammal trainer do?

A: My job is basically to train sea mammals. You've probably seen dolphins
5 jump into the air, whales wave hello, and seals dance. That's what we teach
them to do. (①) But mostly, we take care of the animals. (②) We prepare
their food, clean their tanks, and monitor their health. (③) For example,
animals are taught to stay still during medical procedures, such as getting
blood samples and taking x-rays. (④)

Q: How do you train animals?

A: We teach them tricks using _____(A)_____.
For example, to make dolphins jump, we first teach
them to touch a target like a red ball on the water's
surface. Then, we start raising the target. We repeat the
15 process over and over again until they jump high enough to
hit the target 18 feet above the surface.

Q: _____(B)_____

A: Giving rewards works well. We reward the animals by giving
food and toys, saying the word "good," or rubbing
20 them. But for an action to be taught, the reward
must be given at the exact moment when they perform it.

Q: Do you like your job?

A: Of course I do! Training and caring for animals is hard but very rewarding.
I can proudly say I'm their teacher, parent, and best friend!

1 **What is the interview mainly about?**

   a. Unusual animal behavior

   b. The popularity of dolphin shows

   c. Working as a trainer of sea mammals

   d. The importance of training sea mammals

2 **Where would the following sentences best fit?**

Sometimes we train them to help us care for them.

   a. ①   *b.* ②   *c.* ③   *d.* ④

3 **What is the best choice for blank (A)?**

   a. small steps

   b. unique signals

   c. plenty of praise

   d. a variety of tools

4 **What is the best choice for blank (B)?**

   a. How can you be friendly with the animals?

   b. What do you give the animals when they want to play?

   c. What is your secret to teaching the animals to do what you want?

   d. How do you punish the animals when they don't follow your orders?

5 **While teaching a trick, when must the reward be given to the animals?**

_____

6 **What is NOT true according to the interview?**

   a. Trainers are responsible for keeping the animals healthy.

   b. When the animals get medical checkups, trainers let them move freely.

   c. Trainers train dolphins to jump high by making them hit a target.

   d. Touching is sometimes used as a reward for the animals.

STRATEGIC ORGANIZER

Fill in the blanks with the correct words.

A Sea Mammal Trainer

- Prepares food, cleans _____, cares for the animals' health
- Teaches animals _____ using small steps
- Gives the animals _____ like food, toys, praise, or _____
- Works as the animals' teacher, parent, and best friend

| rubbing | tricks | present | tanks | rewards |

★ EXPANDING KNOWLEDGE ★

Encyclopedia Contents: Sea Mammals

1. Classification
 1.1 Whales and dolphins
 1.2 Seals, sea lions, and walruses
 1.3 Sea cows
 1.4 Polar bears and otters
2. Body features
 2.1 Body shape
 2.2 Tails and fins
 2.3 Fur

3. Habitats
 3.1 Ocean
 3.2 Coastal areas
4. Threats
 4.1 Hunting
 4.2 Competition for food
 4.3 Habitat loss
 4.4 Pollution
 4.5 Global warming

1 Write the correct highlighted word next to its definition.

1) a part at the back of an animal: _____

2) someone or something that could cause danger or harm: _____

3) the action or process of adding harmful substances to the environment: _____

2 Write T if the statement is true or F if it's false.

1) Sea lions are more similar to sea cows than they are to seals.

2) Sea mammals live in the sea and on land next to the sea.

VOCABULARY REVIEW

A Write the correct word next to its definition.

repeat	reward	mammal	prepare	tank

1 to make something ready: _____

2 to do the same thing again: _____

3 something you get after you work hard: _____

4 an animal that gives birth to its young and feeds them with milk: _____

B Find the word that has a similar meaning to the underlined word.

1 It's hard to teach an old dog new <u>tricks</u>.

 a. owners   *b.* hunts   *c.* jumps   *d.* skills

2 The police <u>monitor</u> people who are thought to be criminals.

 a. watch   *b.* greet   *c.* catch   *d.* shoot

C Choose the best word to complete each sentence.

1 That river is the natural _____ of several species of fish.

 a. habitat   *b.* life   *c.* product   *d.* resource

2 Don't stand _____; go ahead and move around a bit.

 a. up   *b.* straight   *c.* out   *d.* still

3 The poor cat had no owner to _____ him.

 a. catch up with   *b.* care for   *c.* agree with   *d.* apply for

4 The accident happened in April, but I can't remember the _____ date.

 a. wrong   *b.* basic   *c.* exact   *d.* pleasant

TECHNOLOGY

Ubiquitous Healthcare

If you're sick, you go to see a doctor. However, if you live in a rural area with no hospitals, visiting a doctor isn't easy. But thanks to newly developed networking technology, you can get proper medical care anywhere and anytime. This technology is *Ubiquitous Healthcare, also known as U-Health.

5   ① For patients to use this service, they need to wear sensors on various body parts, including their wrists, chest, and waist, during their daily lives. ② Some patients complain that wearing sensors is uncomfortable. ③ The sensors regularly collect important data such as body temperature, heartbeat, and blood pressure. ④ The collected data is sent to a healthcare

10 center through a wireless networking system. If serious changes are detected, the system will send an alert to doctors. Then doctors study the data to understand the health of the patient and suggest treatments or even diet changes. It is just like _____(A)_____!

Therefore, this system can be helpful for older people who are not able

15 to easily travel a long distance to visit a doctor. In addition, it saves the time and money that people spend to get a simple medical checkup.

U-Health is still a new and developing technology, but in the near future, people may no longer need to go to see a doctor. With U-Health systems, the doctor will come to you!

*ubiquitous: being everywhere at once

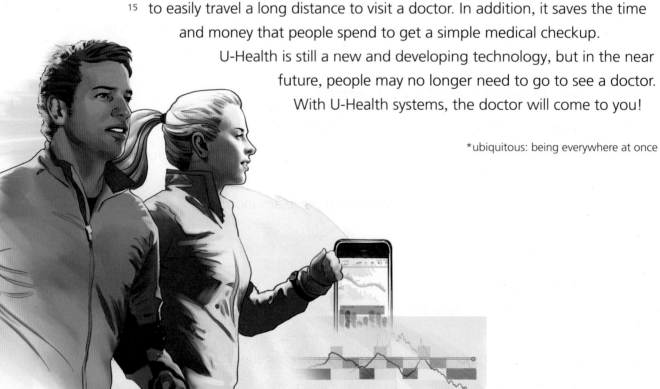

1 What is the passage mainly about?

    a. An ideal welfare system

    b. A new type of healthcare service

    c. Reasons for taking care of the elderly

    d. The history of ubiquitous computing systems

2 With the help of networking technology, U-Health makes it possible for us to _____ .

3 Which sentence is NOT needed in the passage?

    a. ①   *b.* ②   *c.* ③   *d.* ④

4 What is the best choice for blank (A)?

    a. meeting a new friend

    b. being treated as a VIP

    c. wasting time and energy

    d. visiting a doctor in person

5 Who is NOT talking about his or her use of the U-Health service?

    a. Jessica: Wherever I go, I wear a sensor on my wrist.

    b. Nick: My U-Health doctor told me to get some exercise.

    c. Kay: I don't have to visit a doctor to check my blood pressure.

    d. Chris: I have to email my personal data to my doctor regularly.

6 Write T if the statement is true or F if it's false.

    1) When the doctors are given an alert, they quickly go to visit the patients.

    2) U-Health will be helpful for old people who live in the countryside.

Fill in the blanks with the correct words.

| Ubiquitous Healthcare | — A system to get _____ help without seeing a doctor |

How it works
- The patient wears body _____ that collect information.
- The data is collected and sent to a healthcare center.
- Doctors study the data and make _____ to the patient.

How it helps
- Makes it easier and _____ for faraway patients to be checked out by a doctor

| sensors | cheaper | medical | wireless | suggestions |

★ EXPANDING KNOWLEDGE ★

Encyclopedia Contents: Wireless Communications

1. Elements
   1.1 Signals, transmitters, receivers
   1.2 Technologies
       1.2.1 Radio wireless technologies
       1.2.2 Electromagnetic wireless technologies
2. Wireless services
   2.1 Wireless Fidelity (WiFi)
   2.2 Global Positioning System (GPS)
   2.3 Satellite television

3. Applications of wireless technology
   3.1 Mobile telephones
   3.2 Wireless data communications
   3.3 Wireless energy transfer
   3.4 Wireless medical technologies
   3.5 Computer interface devices
       3.5.1 Wireless computer mice, keyboards, etc.

1 Write the correct highlighted word next to its definition.

1) the act of moving from one place to another: _____

2) related to a machine that is sent into space and orbits the earth: _____

3) a series of electrical waves that carry sounds, images, or messages: _____

2 Write T if the statement is true or F if it's false.

1) GPS is not accessible without using wired Internet.

2) It is possible to send and receive energy through wireless technology.

VOCABULARY REVIEW

A Write the correct word next to its definition.

rural	sensor	chest	complain	temperature

1 being in the countryside: _____

2 the degree of how hot a person's body is: _____

3 to express that you're unhappy or not satisfied with something: _____

4 a device which reacts to certain physical conditions, such as heat or light: _____

B Find the word that has a similar meaning to the underlined word.

1 This test is used to <u>detect</u> the alcohol level in a person's blood.

   a. protect   *b.* increase   *c.* find   *d.* lose

2 I <u>suggest</u> that you write about problems related to environmental pollution.

   a. allow   *b.* advise   *c.* provide   *d.* prevent

C Choose the best word to complete each sentence.

1 When people get excited, their _____ gets faster.

   a. blood   *b.* heartbeat   *c.* waist   *d.* wrist

2 Police _____ blood samples for DNA tests.

   a. visited   *b.* spent   *c.* collected   *d.* produced

3 The subway was so crowded that I felt very _____.

   a. fresh   *b.* healthy   *c.* convenient   *d.* uncomfortable

4 When a flood _____ was announced, people began to leave the area.

   a. note   *b.* saying   *c.* alert   *d.* expression

PSYCHOLOGY

False Memories

Our memory is formed from what we have seen, heard, and experienced. But sometimes, people remember things or events that never actually happened. This is called false memory. How does it happen?

5 A psychologist named Elizabeth Loftus carried out an experiment to find out. (①) In the experiment, researchers made a fake advertisement for Disneyland. (②) After seeing it, the participants were asked if they remembered meeting Bugs Bunny at Disneyland when they were young. (③) About 35% of the people answered that they did. (④) What's more, some of them said that they could remember details, such as hugging him

10 or taking photos with him. However, this is impossible because Bugs Bunny is not a Disney character!

So how are these false memories created? According to the research, they are easily created by combining our actual memories with false suggestions. When people are given false information, such as

15 _____(A)_____, they imagine the situation in their minds. Later, what they imagined is mixed with their real memories, like visiting Disneyland. And then it becomes hard to distinguish memories of real events from memories of the suggested ones. Finally, people believe that they really experienced the suggested events, and they create a false memory.

20 In fact, a false memory is not the same as lying. It's just the memory that is false. So think about your own memories. Are you sure all of them are real?

1 **What is the best title for the passage?**

  a. How Real Are Your Memories?

  b. How to Improve Your Memory

  c. The Most Popular Disney Character

  d. Elizabeth Loftus' Interesting Experiment

2 **Where would the following sentence best fit?**

> It showed the cartoon character Bugs Bunny shaking hands with people there.

  a. ①   *b.* ②   *c.* ③   *d.* ④

3 **Why can't we see Bugs Bunny at Disneyland?**

  _____

4 **Match the sequence of how false memories are made in order from (A) to (C).**

> False suggestion → ___(A)___ → ___(B)___ → ___(C)___ → False memory

  1) (A) •   • *a.* Confusion

  2) (B) •   • *b.* Imagination

  3) (C) •   • *c.* Mixing with real memories

5 **What is the best choice for blank (A)?**

  a. making the advertisement

  b. participating in the experiment

  c. watching Bugs Bunny cartoons

  d. meeting Bugs Bunny at Disneyland

6 **Write T if the statement is true or F if it's false.**

  1) About a third of the participants claimed that they had seen Bugs Bunny at Disneyland.

  2) Those who answered that they met Bugs Bunny at Disneyland were telling a lie.

Fill in the blanks with the correct words.

Not all of the things we remember really happened. Research has shown that it is possible to create _____ memories. This happens when a person is given false information and _____ it with his or her real memories. For example, in one experiment, psychologist Elizabeth Loftus _____ to the participants that they might have met Bugs Bunny at Disneyland. Even though this is impossible, as Bugs Bunny is not a Disney character, many people _____ that this really happened to them.

> combines   distinguishes   suggested   believed   false

★ *EXPANDING KNOWLEDGE* ★

Encyclopedia Contents: Memory

1. Function
   1.1 Storing
   1.2 Recalling
2. Short-term Memory
3. Long-term Memory
4. Factors that affect memory
   4.1 Odors
   4.2 Sounds
   4.3 Emotions
   4.4 Previous knowledge

5. Causes of memory disorder
   5.1 Brain injury
   5.2 Stress
   5.3 Aging
   5.4 Disease
6. Improving memory
   6.1 Healthy diet
   6.2 Stress reduction
   6.3 Exercise
   6.4 Enough sleep

1 Write the correct highlighted word next to its definition.

1) the job that something or someone does: _____

2) damage or harm done to a person or animal: _____

3) an illness that affects one's physical or mental condition: _____

2 Write T if the statement is true or F if it's false.

1) Strong smells can influence your memory.

2) Mental fitness as well as physical fitness improves memory.

VOCABULARY REVIEW

A Write the correct word next to its definition.

participant	combine	experience	memory	detail

1 to join two or more things together: _____

2 something that you recall from the past: _____

3 one of the many small facts about something: _____

4 someone who is involved in an activity or event: _____

B Find the word that has a similar meaning to the underlined word.

1 The movie is based on an <u>actual</u> historical event.

   a. imaginary   *b.* difficult   *c.* false   *d.* real

2 She is doing some <u>research</u> on animal behavior.

   a. rest   *b.* studies   *c.* exercises   *d.* reactions

C Choose the best word to complete each sentence.

1 The _____ of cigarette smoke is strong in this room.

   a. memory   *b.* odor   *c.* sound   *d.* factor

2 The plan is unrealistic, so it would be impossible to _____.

   a. give away   *b.* put on   *c.* carry out   *d.* find out

3 The police caught them selling _____ diamonds.

   a. fake   *b.* delicious   *c.* popular   *d.* common

4 Young children are often unable to _____ dreams from reality.

   a. choose   *b.* present   *c.* propose   *d.* distinguish

Before Reading
When you think of spinach, tomatoes, or blueberries, what comes to mind?

Superfoods

Spinach, pumpkins, tomatoes, blueberries, etc.
These plain fruits and vegetables all have something
in common: They are superfoods! Most superfoods
are fruits and vegetables that have bright colors.

5 _____(A)_____, certain fish like salmon, and
nuts like walnuts are also included among these
types of foods.

So what makes these foods so "super"? (①) According to Dr.
Steven Pratt, who first used the term, these foods are so highly nutritious
10 that they have great health benefits. (②) They give us lots of energy and
help us fight illnesses and aging. (③) So, you can even lose weight by
eating them regularly. (④)

Popeye's favorite food, spinach, is one of the best superfoods. This
isn't surprising, because spinach is high in vitamin A, vitamin C, and various
15 minerals. These strengthen our immune system. Blueberries, meanwhile, are
high in vitamin C and *antioxidants. These nutrients can protect us from
cancer and improve our vision. And salmon contains high levels of omega-3
fatty acids, which help prevent heart disease.

However, not everyone agrees with the idea of superfoods.
20 ① Some nutrition experts argue that the health benefits of these foods are
overestimated. ② So you should eat more superfoods for your health.
③ Some also warn that it's not good to eat only superfoods and nothing
else. ④ No matter how healthy superfoods are, it is important to always
have a balanced diet!

*antioxidant: a substance that protects the body from cancer

1 What is the passage mainly about?

a. Some nutrient-rich foods

b. The benefits of a balanced diet

c. The side effects of taking too many vitamins

d. Why people should eat fruits and vegetables

2 What is the best choice for blank (A)?

a. Instead

b. However

c. Therefore

d. In addition

3 Where would the following sentence best fit in the 2nd paragraph?

And these foods are not only healthy but also low in calories.

a. ①

b. ②

c. ③

d. ④

4 How can vitamin C and antioxidants in blueberries help us?

_____

5 Which sentence is NOT needed in the passage?

a. ①

b. ②

c. ③

d. ④

6 What is NOT mentioned about superfoods?

a. Who first used the term

b. What they are good for

c. Which nutrients they contain

d. How many there are

Fill in the blanks with the correct words.

Superfoods	
Benefits	• Make us feel _____ and look young • Help us fight _____ and lose weight
Nutrients	• Spinach: vitamins and _____ that make our immune system strong • Blueberries: vitamin C and antioxidants that protect us from cancer • Salmon: omega-3 fatty acids that prevent heart disease
Oppositions	• Superfoods are _____. • It's not good to only eat superfoods.

> diseases　improve　minerals　energetic　overvalued

★ EXPANDING KNOWLEDGE ★

Encyclopedia Contents: Food and Nutrition

1. Nutrients
   1.1 Carbohydrates: grains, bread, etc.
   1.2 Protein: meat, milk, eggs, fish, etc.
   1.3 Fat: animal fat, vegetable fat
   1.4 Minerals
   1.5 Vitamins
      1.5.1 Water-soluble: B, C
      1.5.1 Fat-soluble: A, D, E, K

2. Healthy diets
3. Illnesses caused by improper nutrition
   3.1 Deficiency
      3.1.1 Starvation, skin disease, etc.
   3.2 Excess
      3.2.1 Obesity, diabetes, heart disease, etc.

1 Write the correct highlighted word next to its definition.

1) a lack of something that is needed: _____

2) not suitable to a particular situation: _____

3) the condition of being severely overweight: _____

2 Write T if the statement is true or F if it's false.

1) Some types of vitamins can be dissolved in water.

2) Excessive consumption of nutrients can lead to skin disease.

VOCABULARY REVIEW

A Write the correct word next to its definition.

nutritious	term	immune system	aging	expert

1 the process of getting old: _____

2 a word or expression that has a certain meaning: _____

3 full of things that help the body to grow properly: _____

4 the organs and processes that protect your body against diseases: _____

B Find the word that has a similar meaning to the underlined word.

1 He is hopeful that he will recover from his <u>illness</u>.

    a. pain   *b.* sadness   *c.* surgery   *d.* disease

2 The museum <u>contains</u> a number of original works of art.

    a. sells   *b.* has   *c.* buys   *d.* displays

C Choose the best word to complete each sentence.

1 Staring at a computer monitor for a long time harms your _____.

    a. spirit   *b.* weight   *c.* vision   *d.* look

2 Many people suffered from _____ after the war.

    a. obesity   *b.* starvation   *c.* nutrition   *d.* question

3 I've started working out to _____ my arm muscles.

    a. reduce   *b.* include   *c.* weaken   *d.* strengthen

4 You don't need any advanced knowledge to do this job; you just need _____ common sense.

    a. special   *b.* professional   *c.* deficient   *d.* plain

Oxfam

Do you know what Oxfam is? Although the name may remind you of an ox or a family, it has nothing to do with them. In fact, Oxfam is an international organization that fights global poverty in more than 90 countries around the world.

The name "Oxfam" comes from the Oxford Committee for Famine Relief. It was founded by a group of citizens of Oxford in 1942, during World War II. Its first mission was to collect food and clothes for families whose lives had been ruined by the war.

These days, Oxfam focuses more on solving the causes of poverty to relieve famine. The organization helps people not only by giving them _____(A)_____ assistance such as providing food and clothes, but also by offering them

20 _____(B)_____ solutions to escape poverty. For example, it helps poor children get a good education for a better future. It also loans money to poor people to start small businesses.

In addition, Oxfam runs shops around the world. (①) These stores sell donated secondhand goods and, more importantly, a variety of products made in developing countries. (②) These items are sold through fair trade

25 to help boost the quality of life in the communities that produce them. (③) Also, the profits are used to fund Oxfam's relief activities. (④)

1 **What is the best title for the passage?**

a. Oxfam Gives Hope to the Poor
b. Oxfam: A Rising Fashion Brand
c. A Welfare System for Poor People
d. Oxfam: A Smart Consumer's Choice

2 **What was Oxfam's primary mission when it was founded?**

_____

3 **What is the best pair for blanks (A) and (B)?**

	(A)		(B)
a.	practical	—	unrealistic
b.	financial	—	non-financial
c.	short-term	—	long-term
d.	indirect	—	direct

4 **Where would the following sentence best fit?**

> Among them are handicrafts, clothing, toys, and musical instruments.

a. ①   b. ②   c. ③   d. ④

5 **What is NOT mentioned as one of Oxfam's activities?**

a. Enabling poor children to receive education
b. Helping poor people to start businesses
c. Selling goods made in poor countries
d. Building shelters for the poor

6 **Write T if the statement is true or F if it's false.**

1) Oxfam works with more than 90 organizations.
2) Oxfam shops are mainly located in developing countries.

STRATEGIC ORGANIZER

Fill in the blanks with the correct words.

Oxfam – An international association working to end global _____

In the past
• Founded during World War II to _____ famine caused by war

Today
• Focuses on fighting the _____ of poverty
• Helps children get education, loans startup money to poor people
• Runs shops that sell fair trade products to improve people's lives in _____ countries

| profits | poverty | developing | causes | relieve |

★ EXPANDING KNOWLEDGE ★

Encyclopedia Contents: Famine

1. Great famines in history
  1.1 Bengal Famine (India, 1770): drought and crop shortages
  1.2 Great Chinese Famine (China, 1958-1961): failed government policies
2. Causes of famine
  2.1 Natural disasters
  2.2 Unbalanced population
  2.3 War, market crash, etc.

3. Effects of famine
  3.1 Biological effects
    3.1.1 Malnutrition
    3.1.2 Starvation
    3.1.3 Spread of disease
    3.1.4 Death
  3.2 Social effects
    3.2.1 Breakdown of social structure
    3.2.2 Migration

1 Write the correct highlighted word next to its definition.

1) a situation when there is not enough of something: _____

2) a very bad accident that causes great damage or death: _____

3) a long period of time when there is very little or no rain: _____

2 Write T if the statement is true or F if it's false.

1) The great famines in both India and China were man-made disasters.

2) Famine can cause people to move to another country.

A Write the correct word next to its definition.

poverty	loan	assistance	handicraft	run

1 help or support: _____

2 the condition of being poor: _____

3 to be in charge of a business, activity, etc.: _____

4 to lend something like money to someone: _____

B Find the word that has a similar meaning to the underlined word.

1 Everything in the house was completely <u>ruined</u> by the fire.

   a. destroyed   *b.* moved   *c.* changed   *d.* dried

2 Air pollution is one of the most serious <u>global</u> problems.

   a. local   *b.* important   *c.* worldwide   *d.* environmental

C Choose the best word to complete each sentence.

1 I think we should go somewhere warm to _____ the cold weather.

   a. develop   *b.* enjoy   *c.* escape   *d.* improve

2 He likes singing. Singing is one way for him to _____ stress.

   a. operate   *b.* catch   *c.* cause   *d.* relieve

3 She _____ a lot of money to charity every year.

   a. reserves   *b.* donates   *c.* decides   *d.* receives

4 Building a house is a(n) _____ project that requires patience.

   a. long-term   *b.* sudden   *c.* damaged   *d.* exact

Before Reading
Do you have any ideas about how to
reduce carbon dioxide emissions?

Carbon Trading

Global warming is becoming a serious problem. One of its main causes is the emission of carbon dioxide. To solve this problem, "carbon trading" is being used now.

Carbon trading began in 1997 with the Kyoto Protocol. (①)
5　According to this agreement, each country is given a national limit for emissions. (②) The number of credits a company gets depends on its size and area of business. (③) If a company emits less carbon and doesn't use all of its credits, it can trade the remaining credits and make money. (④) But, companies have to cut their emissions over time, because the limits are
10　lowered each year.

Carbon trading is good in that companies can make money from it, so they are likely to try harder to reduce emissions. Also, it gives companies time to reduce their emissions slowly to prevent sudden economic difficulties. However, there are also some problems. For one thing,
15　companies can continue creating pollution. Furthermore, in some cases limits are so high that no trading takes place.

_____(A)_____ these disadvantages, the U.K. is now considering a similar system for households. Under this system, households could trade credits with other households. Do you think it's a good idea?

1 What is the best title for the passage?

    a. How to Get Lots of Carbon Credits

    b. The Disadvantages of Carbon Trading

    c. Serious Problems Caused by Global Warming

    d. Carbon Trading: A Solution to Global Warming?

2 Where would the following sentence best fit?

> Then the government gives "carbon credits" to companies.

    a. ①   *b.* ②   *c.* ③   *d.* ④

3 What decides the number of carbon credits that are given to a company? (Choose two.)

    a. Who owns it

    b. How large it is

    c. What industry it is in

    d. How much money it earns

4 How does carbon trading prevent sudden economic difficulties from affecting companies?

_____

5 What is the best choice for blank (A)?

    a. Due to

    b. Despite

    c. Instead of

    d. According to

6 Write T if the statement is true or F if it's false.

    1) Each government can decide its national limit for emissions.

    2) The U.K. is already applying a carbon trading system for households.

STRATEGIC SUMMARY

Fill in the blanks with the correct words.

Carbon trading started in 1997 to reduce carbon dioxide emissions. It gives companies chances to _____ their carbon credits. It is good because companies can make money by selling their remaining credits. Also, it doesn't force companies to face sudden _____ difficulties, because they can take their time. However, there are two disadvantages. First, companies can keep _____. And sometimes no trading _____.

trade	occurs	polluting	economic	environment

★ EXPANDING KNOWLEDGE ★

English Dictionary

trade ▼	Search

Related Search

export	import	product	industry	international
profit	loss	demand	supply	

Synonyms
- exchange
- business
- deal
- contract
- barter

Collocations
- a trade fair
- a trade barrier
- free trade
- fair trade
- foreign trade
- promote trade

Times News Economy

Write the correct highlighted word next to its definition.

1 relating to several countries: _____

2 money that has been lost by a business: _____

3 to bring products to sell from another country: _____

4 money that you earn by selling things or doing business: _____

VOCABULARY REVIEW

A Write the correct word next to its definition.

cause	emission	trading	lower	main

1 the activity of buying and selling things: _____

2 the act of sending out light, gas, sound, etc.: _____

3 to make something less in amount or quality: _____

4 a person or thing that makes something happen: _____

B Find the word that has a similar meaning to the underlined word.

1 Some experts pointed out that the policy has a few <u>disadvantages</u>.

   a. governments   *b.* drawbacks   *c.* benefits   *d.* opportunities

2 One of the most powerful earthquakes in the world <u>took place</u> in Chile.

   a. changed   *b.* ended   *c.* happened   *d.* followed

C Choose the best word to complete each sentence.

1 There's a _____ on the time I have to complete the project.

   a. limit   *b.* method   *c.* chance   *d.* process

2 Because of environmental _____, some species of fish no longer exist.

   a. advantage   *b.* protection   *c.* help   *d.* pollution

3 I was very shocked to hear of his _____ death.

   a. important   *b.* sudden   *c.* necessary   *d.* special

4 Sarah made more cupcakes with the _____ ingredients.

   a. quiet   *b.* national   *c.* remaining   *d.* serious

MEMO

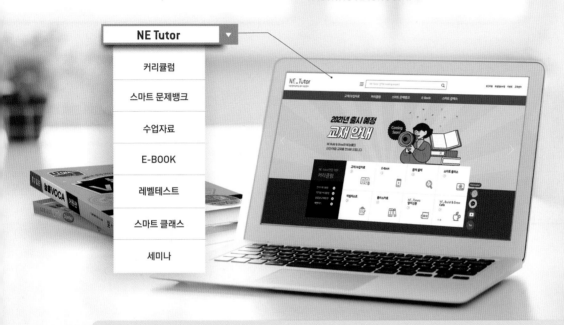

Reading

FORWARD

INTERMEDIATE 1

★ **Word Book** ★

Unit ★ 01 SPORTS

indigenous	형 토착의
organize	동 조직하다
legend	명 전설; 전설적 인물
tribe	명 부족
get together	모이다
take part in	…에 참가하다
fantastic	형 환상적인, 멋진
ceremony	명 의식, 식
parade	명 행진, 퍼레이드
costume	명 의상
skin	명 피부; 가죽
torch	명 햇불
fireworks display	불꽃놀이 대회
last	동 지속되다
athlete	명 운동선수
tug-of-war	명 줄다리기
spear	명 창
canoe	동 카누를 타다
archery	명 양궁
highlight	명 하이라이트, 가장 흥미로운 부분
log	명 통나무
relay race	계주
trunk	명 나무의 몸통
episode	명 사건, 에피소드

show up	나타나다
victory stand	시상대
ranking	몡 순위
celebrate	동 축하하다, 기념하다
native	형 토착민의
unity	몡 단결, 협동
ancient	형 고대의
modern	형 현대의
Paralympics	몡 (pl.) 세계 장애인 올림픽
disabled	형 장애를 가진
symbol	몡 상징
presentation	몡 제출; 수여, 증정
host	몡 주최국, 주최측
committee	몡 위원회
properly	부 제대로
injury	몡 부상, 상처
consist of	…로 구성되다

Unit ★ 02 FOOD

shaped	형 …의 모양의
pastry	몡 페이스트리
crispy	형 바삭바삭한
attack	동 공격하다

dig	동 파다
underground	형 지하의
get into	…에 들어가다
basement	명 지하
flag	명 기, 깃발
bite	동 물다
doubt	동 의심하다 명 의심
appear	동 나타나다
uncertain	형 불분명한
army	명 군대
destroy	동 파괴하다
defeat	동 패배시키다, 물리치다
enemy	명 적
introduction	명 도입, 전래
grain	명 곡물
wheat	명 밀
rye	명 호밀
oats	명 (pl.) 귀리
ingredient	명 재료, 성분
yeast	명 이스트, 효모
nutrient	명 영양소, 영양분
carbohydrate	명 탄수화물
dietary fiber	식이성 섬유
substance	명 물질
custom	명 관습, 풍습
grind	동 갈다

top hat	서양의 남성 정장용 모자
icon	⑲ 우상, 아이콘
meatpacker	⑲ 정육업자
barrel	⑲ (목재 · 금속으로 된 대형) 통
mark	⑧ (이름 · 표시 등을) …에 적다
stand for	…을 나타내다
nickname	⑲ 별명
political	⑲ 정치적인
cartoon	⑲ 만화
appearance	⑲ 외모; 등장, 출현
beard	⑲ 턱수염
recruit	⑧ (신병 등을) 모집하다
stare	⑧ 응시하다
point	⑧ 가리키다
phrase	⑲ 문구
beneath	㉓ 아래에
popular culture	대중문화
logo	⑲ 로고, 상징
resemble	⑧ 닮다
president	⑲ 대통령
character	⑲ 등장인물
goodhearted	⑲ 친절한, 마음씨가 고운
represent	⑧ 대표하다
cartoonist	⑲ 만화가

waistcoat	몡 조끼
nevertheless	悜 그럼에도 불구하고

Unit ★ 04 BOYS & GIRLS

item	몡 물품, 품목
true	瀀 사실의; …에 적용되는[해당하는]
reality	몡 현실
when it comes to	…에 관한 한
planet	몡 행성
mall	몡 쇼핑몰
directly	悜 곧장
search for	…을 찾다
best price	최저 가격
check out	확인하다; 살펴보다
discount	몡 할인
a variety of	다양한, 여러 가지의
perfume	몡 향수
scholar	몡 학자
mission	몡 임무
complete	悧 완료하다, 끝마치다
recreational	瀀 오락의
matter	몡 문제
lounge	몡 휴게실, 라운지

gender	똉 성, 성별
must have	똉 꼭 필요한, 반드시 가져야 하는
wander	똉 거닐다
male	똉 남자
female	똉 여자
masculine	똉 남성의
feminine	똉 여성의
individual	똉 개인의
race	똉 인종
mate	똉 친구, 짝
spouse	똉 배우자
population	똉 인구
equality	똉 평등
identity	똉 정체
discrimination	똉 차별
stereotype	똉 고정 관념
quality	똉 특징, 특성
associated with	…와 관련된
unfair	똉 부당한, 불공평한
treatment	똉 대우

Unit ★ 05 LITERATURE

rule	똉 통치하다

cruel	혱 잔혹한, 무자비한
place	동 두다, 놓다
pole	명 막대기, 장대
bow	동 절하다
punish	동 벌하다
crossbow	명 석궁
shoot	동 쏘다
arrow	명 화살
hesitant	혱 주저하는
beg	동 간청하다
ignore	동 무시하다
faith	명 믿음
skilled	혱 숙련된, 노련한
aim	명 목표; 겨냥, 조준
whiz	명 윙(화살이 내는 소리)
cheer	동 환호하다
calmly	븻 침착하게
bravery	명 용기
arrest	동 체포하다
evil	혱 사악한
moral	혱 도덕적인
wicked	혱 못된, 사악한
mean	혱 못된, 심술궂은
intend	동 의도하다
courage	명 용기
courageous	혱 용감한
challenge	명 도전

curious	휑 호기심 많은
generous	휑 너그러운
heroic	휑 영웅다운
fearless	휑 두려움을 모르는
adventurous	휑 모험심이 강한
shy	휑 수줍음을 많이 타는
timid	휑 소심한
cowardly	휑 겁이 많은
spirit	휑 정신, 영혼; (특정한 유형의) 사람
attempt	휑 시도
behavior	휑 행동
put on a brave face	자신 있는 척하다
cheat	동 속이다

Unit ★ 06 MUSIC

composer	휑 작곡가
brilliant	휑 뛰어난
lifetime	휑 일생, 생애
hire	동 고용하다
emperor	휑 황제
royal	휑 국왕의
court	휑 법정; 궁궐
chief	휑 (계급·직급상) 최고의

classical	휑 고전적인; (음악이) 클래식의
rumor	똉 소문
genius	똉 천재성
jealous	휑 시기하는; 질투심 많은
poison	똉 독약 똉 독살하다
common	휑 흔한; 평범한
murder	똉 살해하다
murderer	똉 살인자
die of	…로 죽다
natural cause	자연적 원인
annual	휑 매년의, 연례의
myth	똉 신화; (근거 없는) 이야기
compare A with B	A를 B와 비교하다
influence	똉 영향을 미치다
period	똉 기간; 시대
medieval	휑 중세의
practice	똉 관습
era	똉 시대
contemporary	휑 동시대의; 현대의
instrument	똉 악기
string	똉 현악기
woodwind	똉 목관악기
brass	똉 금관악기
percussion	똉 타악기

coat	몡 외투; 상의
gown	몡 (여성의) 드레스; (의사 등이 입는) 가운
perform	동 행하다, 수행하다
surgery	몡 수술
stare at	…을 빤히 쳐다보다, 응시하다
be related to	…와 관계가 있다
afterimage	몡 잔상
certain	혱 확실한; 어떤
cell	몡 세포
background	몡 배경
floating	혱 떠 있는
shape	몡 모양, 형태
opposite	혱 반대의 몡 반대(되는 것)
prevent	동 막다, 방지하다
concentrate on	…에 집중하다
stain	몡 얼룩
stand out	쉽게 눈에 띄다
vision	몡 시력; 환상, 상상
view	몡 견해; 시야
sight	몡 시력; 광경
visible	혱 보이는, 알아볼 수 있는
visual	혱 시각의
inspire	동 고무하다, 격려하다
illusion	몡 환상

normal	형 보통의, 정상적인
20-20 vision	완벽한[정상] 시력
ordinary	형 보통의, 일상적인

Unit★08 HISTORY

popularity	명 인기
unpopular	형 인기 없는
introduce	동 소개하다; (처음으로) 전하다[들여오다]
inspire	동 격려하다; 불어넣다, 고취시키다
creativity	명 창의력, 창조력
provide	동 공급하다, 주다
region	명 지방, 지역
spread	동 퍼지다 명 확산, 전파
throughout	전 …의 도처에
discuss	동 논의하다, 토론하다
topic	명 화제, 주제
politics	명 정치
philosophy	명 철학
intellectual	형 지적인
long-lasting	형 오래 지속되는
youth	명 젊은이
institution	명 기관, 단체
social	형 사회적인

interaction	명 상호작용
cultivation	명 경작, 재배
in order	순으로, 순서대로
process	명 과정
roast	동 볶다
grind	동 갈다
brew	동 끓이다
benefit	명 이점
improvement	명 향상
rich	형 부유한; …이 풍부한
antioxidant	명 산화 방지제
risk	명 위험
blood pressure	혈압
dehydration	명 탈수; 탈수증
fair trade	공정 거래

Unit ★ 09 FESTIVALS

powder	명 가루
stranger	명 낯선[모르는] 사람
pistol	명 총
spray	동 뿌리다
festival	명 축제
harvest	명 수확, 추수

decorate	⑧ 장식하다, 꾸미다
colorful	⑱ 형형색색의, 다채로운
unique	⑱ 독특한; 고유한
represent	⑧ 나타내다
harmony	⑲ 조화
worship	⑧ 숭배하다
wicked	⑱ 사악한
bonfire	⑲ 모닥불
end up	결국 ···하게 되다
unite	⑧ 결합하다, 통합하다
obey	⑧ 복종하다
participate in	···에 참여하다
purpose	⑲ 목적
celebration	⑲ 기념 행사
entertainment	⑲ 오락
feature	⑲ 특징, 특색
firework	⑲ (*pl.*) 불꽃놀이
beverage	⑲ 음료
costume	⑲ 의상, 복장
religious	⑱ 종교적인
literature	⑲ 문학
seasonal	⑱ 계절적인

Unit ★ 10 PLACES

attraction	몡 명소, 명물
locate	통 (특정 위치에) 두다, 설치하다
bank	몡 둑
priceless	휑 값을 매길 수 없는, 귀중한
including	젠 …을 포함하여
impressionist	휑 인상주의의 몡 인상파 화가
period	몡 기간; 시대
railroad	몡 철도
eventually	뷔 결과적으로
abandon	통 버리다
fit	통 맞다
platform	몡 플랫폼, 승강장
house	통 보관하다, 소장하다
collection	몡 수집품, 소장품
sculpture	몡 조각(품)
convert	통 전환하다, 개조하다
distinctive	휑 독특한
elegant	휑 우아한
domed	휑 반구형의
ceiling	몡 천장
view	통 보다
entrance	몡 입구
chest	몡 가슴; 상자
former	휑 이전의

portrait	몡 초상화
landscape	몡 풍경화
still life	정물화
impressionism	몡 인상주의
expressionism	몡 표현주의
cubism	몡 입체파
realism	몡 사실주의
metropolitan	혱 대도시의

Unit ★ 11 ENTERTAINMENT

orchestra	몡 오케스트라, 관현악단
perform	동 연주하다
performance	몡 연주
at the same time	동시에
giant	혱 거대한
dramatic	혱 극적인; 인상적인
over and over	여러 번 되풀이하여
cleverly	旱 영리하게; 솜씨 좋게
cymbal	몡 (pl.) (악기) 심벌즈
produce	동 만들어내다
grand	혱 웅장한
complicated	혱 복잡한
classical	혱 고전적인; (음악이) 클래식의

medley	몡 메들리
amazed	혱 놀란
amazing	혱 놀라운
original	혱 원래의
cheer	동 환호하다
entertaining	혱 재미있는, 즐거운
dress up	분장시키다
brand-new	혱 아주 새로운, 신품의
repetitive	혱 반복적인
amusement	몡 재미, 오락
exhibition	몡 전시, 전시회
broadcast	동 방송하다 몡 방송
impression	몡 인상, 느낌
audience	몡 청중, 관중; 관람객
pleasing	혱 즐거운
delightful	혱 정말 기분 좋은
fascinating	혱 매력적인; 아주 재미있는
boring	혱 지루한
depressing	혱 우울한
dull	혱 따분한
uninteresting	혱 재미없는
artwork	몡 예술품
object	몡 물건, 물체

Unit ★ 12 ANIMALS

expression	몡 표현
completely	뿐 완전히
phrase	몡 구, 구절
suggest	동 제안하다; 시사하다, 암시하다
species	몡 (생물의) 종
disappear	동 사라지다
disappearance	몡 사라짐
extinct	뼹 멸종된
paradise	몡 천국; 낙원
isolated	뼹 외딴; 고립된
rest	몡 나머지
enemy	몡 적
seed	몡 씨, 씨앗
gradually	뿐 서서히
evolve	동 발달하다; 진화하다
bound	뼹 …에 발이 묶인
increase	동 증가하다
weigh	동 무게가 …이다
explorer	몡 탐험가
name	동 이름을 지어주다
habitat	몡 서식지
destroy	동 파괴하다
encounter	동 접하다, 마주치다
remain	동 (없어지지 않고) 남다

fate	몡 운명
imaginary	혱 가공의, 상상의
convenient	혱 편리한
target	몡 대상, 표적
in danger of	…할 위험이 있는
bite	동 물다, 베어 물다
tough	혱 힘든; 단단한
shell	몡 껍데기, 껍질
exit	동 나가다
dropping	몡 낙하; (*pl.*) (동물의) 똥
fortunately	부 다행스럽게도
turkey	몡 칠면조
survive	동 살아남다, 생존하다
affect	동 …에 영향을 미치다
ecosystem	몡 생태계
prevent	동 막다
extinction	몡 멸종

Unit ★ *13* ARCHITECTURE

discomfort	몡 불편
comfort	몡 편안함
uncomfortable	혱 불편한
unique	혱 독특한

reversible	⑱ 거꾸로 할 수 있는
destiny	⑲ 운명
loft	⑲ 다락방; 아파트
sphere	⑲ 구
cube	⑲ 정육면체, 입방체
indoor	⑱ 실내의
flat	⑱ 평평한
bumpy	⑱ 울퉁불퉁한
unexpected	⑱ 예상치 못한, 뜻밖의
feel around	여기저기 더듬거리다
crawl	⑧ 기어가다
balance	⑲ 균형
dizzy	⑱ 어지러운
unusual	⑱ 특이한
latest	⑱ 최신의
trend	⑲ 경향
smooth	⑱ 매끄러운
surface	⑲ 표면
have a hard time v-ing	…하느라 고생하다
weird	⑱ 기이한
specific	⑱ 구체적인
equal	⑱ 동등한
personality	⑲ 성격
identity	⑲ 독자성
absolute	⑱ 완전한, 완벽한
odd	⑱ 이상한, 특이한
peculiar	⑱ 이상한, 별난

remarkable	휑 놀라운, 주목할 만한
rare	휑 드문, 진기한
typical	휑 전형적인
common	휑 흔한
ordinary	휑 보통의
quantity	휑 양
quality	휑 질; 특성, 특색

Unit★14 CULTURE

library	휑 도서관
borrow	동 빌리다, 대출하다
found	동 설립하다
founder	휑 창립자, 설립자
lend	동 빌려주다
feminist	휑 페미니스트, 남녀평등주의자
aggressive	휑 공격적인
vegetarian	휑 채식주의자
sensitive	휑 섬세한; 예민한
negative	휑 부정적인
prejudice	휑 편견
addicted	휑 중독된
addiction	휑 중독
respect	동 존경하다

misunderstand	⑧ 오해하다
viewpoint	⑲ 관점
objective	⑲ 객관적인
subjective	⑲ 주관적인
optimistic	⑲ 낙관적인
pessimistic	⑲ 비관적인
bias	⑲ 편견
angle	⑲ 각도; 시각, 관점
outlook	⑲ 관점
perspective	⑲ 관점, 시각
standpoint	⑲ 견지, 관점
critical	⑲ 비판적인
narrow	⑲ (관점이) 좁은, 편협한
expect	⑧ 기대하다
belief	⑲ 믿음, 생각

Unit ⋆ 15 JOBS

mammal	⑲ 포유동물
trainer	⑲ 훈련자; 조련사
train	⑧ 훈련하다
basically	⑨ 기본적으로
dolphin	⑲ 돌고래
whale	⑲ 고래

wave	통 (손·팔을) 흔들다
seal	명 바다표범, 물개
take care of	…을 돌보다
tank	명 탱크; 물통
monitor	통 감시하다, 관리하다
still	형 가만히 있는
medical	형 의학의
procedure	명 절차; 수술, 시술
trick	명 속임수; 재주, 곡예
target	명 목표; 목표물
surface	명 표면, 수면
raise	통 들어 올리다
repeat	통 반복하다
reward	명 보상 통 보상하다
rewarding	형 보람 있는
rub	통 문지르다; 쓰다듬다
care for	…을 보살피다, 돌보다
proudly	부 자랑스럽게
signal	명 신호
responsible	형 책임이 있는
checkup	명 건강진단
classification	명 분류
sea lion	바다사자
walrus	명 바다코끼리
sea cow	바다소
polar bear	북극곰
otter	명 수달

tail	몡 꼬리
fin	몡 지느러미
fur	몡 털
habitat	몡 서식지
coastal	혱 해안의
threat	몡 협박, 위협
hunting	몡 사냥
competition	몡 경쟁
pollution	몡 오염
global warming	지구온난화

Unit ★16 TECHNOLOGY

rural	혱 시골의, 지방의
thanks to	… 덕분에
develop	동 발달시키다; 개발하다
technology	몡 기술
proper	혱 적절한
medical care	의료, 건강 관리
sensor	몡 센서, 감지기
wrist	몡 손목
chest	몡 가슴
waist	몡 허리
complain	동 불평하다

regularly	ⓟ 정기적으로, 규칙적으로
collect	ⓢ 수집하다
temperature	ⓜ 온도; 체온
heartbeat	ⓜ 심장 박동
blood pressure	혈압
wireless	ⓗ 무선의
detect	ⓢ 발견하다, 감지하다
alert	ⓜ 경계; 경고
suggest	ⓢ 제안하다
treatment	ⓜ 취급; 치료(법)
diet	ⓜ 식이요법
distance	ⓜ 거리
welfare	ⓜ 복지, 행복
elderly	ⓗ 연세가 드신
in person	직접, 스스로
communication	ⓜ 의사소통, 연락
transmitter	ⓜ 송신기, 발신기
receiver	ⓜ 수화기, 수신기
radio	ⓗ 무선의, 무전의
electromagnetic	ⓗ 전자기의
fidelity	ⓜ 정확도, 충실도
Global Positioning System(GPS)	위성 위치 확인 시스템
satellite	ⓗ 위성의
application	ⓜ 적용, 응용
mobile	ⓗ 이동하는, 이동식의
transfer	ⓜ 이동
device	ⓜ 장치, 기구

orbit	동 (지구 등의) 궤도를 돌다
wave	명 파도; 파장, 파동
accessible	형 이용 가능한
wired	형 유선의

Unit ★ 17 PSYCHOLOGY

form	동 형성하다
experience	동 경험하다
actually	부 실제로
actual	형 실제의
false	형 틀린, 사실이 아닌
psychologist	명 심리학자
carry out	…을 수행하다
experiment	명 실험
fake	형 가짜의, 거짓된
advertisement	명 광고
participant	명 참가자
detail	명 세부사항
hug	동 껴안다
research	명 연구, 조사
combine	동 결합하다
suggestion	명 제안; 암시
suggest	동 암시하다

imagine	⑧ 상상하다
imagination	⑲ 상상
situation	⑲ 상황, 처지
mix	⑧ 섞다
distinguish	⑧ 구별하다
shake hands with	…와 악수하다
confusion	⑲ 혼동
claim	⑧ 주장하다
function	⑲ 기능
store	⑧ 저장하다
recall	⑧ 기억해내다
short-term	⑲ 단기의
long-term	⑲ 장기의
factor	⑲ 요소
odor	⑲ 냄새
previous	⑲ 이전의
disorder	⑲ (신체 기능의) 장애
injury	⑲ 부상, 상처
aging	⑲ 노화
reduction	⑲ 감소
illness	⑲ 병
influence	⑧ 영향을 미치다
fitness	⑲ 건강

spinach	몡 시금치
pumpkin	몡 호박
plain	혱 명백한; 평범한
have … in common	(특징 등을) 공통적으로 지니다
salmon	몡 연어
nut	몡 견과
walnut	몡 호두
include	통 포함하다
term	몡 용어, 말
nutritious	혱 영양분이 많은, 영양가가 높은
nutrition	몡 영양(물)
nutrient	몡 영양소, 영양분
benefit	몡 혜택, 이득
regularly	붕 정기적으로, 규칙적으로
mineral	몡 무기물
strengthen	통 강화하다
immune system	면역 체계
meanwhile	붕 그 동안에; 한편
vision	몡 시력
contain	통 …이 들어 있다, 함유되어 있다
fatty acid	지방산
overestimate	통 과대평가하다
balanced	혱 균형 잡힌
side effect	부작용

carbohydrate	몡 탄수화물
protein	혱 난백실
fat	몡 지방
soluble	혱 용해성이 있는
improper	혱 부적절한
deficiency	몡 결핍
starvation	몡 굶주림
excess	몡 과도, 과잉
excessive	혱 과도한, 지나친
obesity	몡 비만
diabetes	몡 당뇨병
suitable	혱 적절한
particular	혱 특정한
severely	몪 심하게
overweight	혱 과체중의
dissolve	동 녹이다, 용해하다
consumption	몡 소비, 소모

Unit★19 SOCIETY

ox	몡 황소
international	혱 국제적인
organization	몡 조직, 단체
poverty	몡 가난

committee	몡 위원회
famine	몡 기근
relief	몡 안도; 구호
relieve	통 완화하다, 줄이다
mission	몡 임무, 사명
ruin	통 파괴하다
assistance	몡 원조, 지원
escape	통 달아나다; 벗어나다
offer	통 제공하다
loan	통 대출하다, (돈을) 빌려주다
secondhand	혱 간접의; 중고의
goods	몡 상품
developing country	개발도상국
boost	통 신장시키다, 북돋우다
community	몡 공동체, 지역 사회
profit	몡 이익, 수익
consumer	몡 소비자
practical	혱 실질적인
financial	혱 재정의, 금융의
handicraft	몡 수공예품
enable	통 …을 가능하게 하다
shelter	몡 피난처, 은신처
drought	몡 가뭄
shortage	몡 부족
government	몡 정부
policy	몡 정책
disaster	몡 재난, 재해

market crash	시장 붕괴
biological	⑧ 생물학적인
malnutrition	⑲ 영양실조
breakdown	⑲ 고장; (시스템 등의) 실패, 와해
structure	⑲ 구조
migration	⑲ 이주, 이동
man-made	⑲ 사람이 만든, 인공의

Unit ★ 20 ENVIRONMENT

emission	⑲ 배출(물)
emit	⑧ 배출하다
carbon dioxide	이산화탄소
trading	⑲ 거래
trade	⑧ 거래하다
protocol	⑲ 의정서, 조약안
agreement	⑲ 협정
national	⑧ 국가의
limit	⑲ 한계; 제한, 허용치
depend on	···에 달려 있다, ···에 의해 결정되다
area	⑲ 지역; 분야
remaining	⑧ 남아 있는
cut	⑧ 자르다; 줄이다
lower	⑧ 내리다, 낮추다

reduce	통 줄이다
economic	형 경제의
take place	일어나다
disadvantage	명 불리한 점, 약점
household	명 가정
carbon credit	탄소 배출권
industry	명 산업
despite	전 …에도 불구하고
apply	통 신청하다; 적용하다
export	통 수출하다 명 수출
import	통 수입하다 명 수입
loss	명 손실; 손실액
lose	통 잃다
demand	명 수요
supply	명 공급
exchange	명 교환 통 교환하다
deal	명 거래 통 거래하다
contract	명 계약 통 계약하다
barter	명 물물교환 통 물건을 교환하다
fair	명 박람회 형 공정한
barrier	명 장애물, 장벽
promote	통 촉진하다

MEMO

Reading FORWARD

INTERMEDIATE 1

★ Answer Key ★

Reading FORWARD

INTERMEDIATE 1

★ Answer Key ★

unit *01* SPORTS

pp. 8-11

★*The Indigenous Olympics*

1 b **2** c **3** b **4** Because they had already left the stadium to enjoy a festival outside. **5** d
6 *1)* F *2)* T

세계의 모든 사람들이 올림픽 경기를 즐긴다. 그러나 브라질에서, 어떤 사람들은 원주민 올림픽이라는 다른 특별한 행사에 더 열광한다. 그것은 1996년에 브라질 축구의 전설적 인물인 펠레에 의해 처음으로 조직되었다. 매년, 40개가 넘는 부족에서 수천 명의 사람들이 내외에 참가하기 위해 모인다.

올림픽 경기처럼, 원주민 올림픽은 환상적인 개막식으로 시작한다. 개막식 동안, 모든 부족들은 행진을 하면서 경기장에 입장한다. 그들은 풀잎 치마와 동물 가죽 장신구를 포함하는 전통 의상을 입고 노래하고 춤을 춘다. (어떤 사람들은 전통 의상을 입고 싶어 하지 않는다.) 식의 마지막에는, 횃불이 점화되고 놀라운 불꽃놀이가 이어진다. 대회는 일주일 동안 계속되고, 선수들은 수영, 줄다리기, 창던지기, 카누, 양궁과 같은 <u>현대 및 전통 경기</u>를 한다. 하이라이트는 통나무 계주인데, 여기서 주자들은 200파운드짜리 나무 몸통을 어깨에 얹고 달린다!

선수들은 대회를 위한 훈련이 되어 있지 않아서, 종종 재미있는 사건들이 생긴다. 한 경주에서, 어떤 주자는 결승선을 지나 계속 달렸다. 또 다른 때에는, 우승자들 중 일부가 메달을 받으러 시상대에 나타나지 않았다. 그들은 장외의 축제를 즐기러 경기장을 이미 떠났던 것이다! 사실 그들에게 메달과 순위는 중요하지 않다. 그러나 모든 부족들이 즐겁게 대회에 참가하고 그들이 함께 모이는 것을 축하한다!

어휘 indigenous[indídʒənəs] 혱 토착의 organize[ɔ́ːrɡənàiz] 통 조직하다 legend[lédʒənd]
혱 전설; *전설적 인물 tribe[traib] 혱 부족 get together 모이다 take part in …에 참가하다
fantastic[fæntǽstik] 혱 환상적인, 멋진 ceremony[sérəmòuni] 혱 의식, 식 parade[pəréid]
혱 행진, 퍼레이드 costume[kástjuːm] 혱 의상 skin[skin] 혱 피부; *가죽 torch[tɔːrtʃ] 혱 횃불
fireworks display 불꽃놀이 대회 last[læst] 통 지속되다 athlete[ǽθliːt] 혱 운동선수
tug-of-war[tʌ́ɡəvwɔ́ːr] 혱 줄다리기 spear[spiər] 혱 창 canoe[kənúː] 통 카누를 타다
archery[áːrtʃəri] 혱 양궁 highlight[háilàit] 혱 하이라이트, 가장 흥미로운 부분 log[lɔ(ː)ɡ]
혱 통나무 relay race 계주 trunk[trʌŋk] 혱 나무의 몸통 episode[épəsòud] 혱 사건, 에피소드
show up 나타나다 victory stand 시상대 ranking[rǽŋkiŋ] 혱 순위 celebrate[séləbrèit]
통 축하하다, 기념하다 [문제] native[néitiv] 혱 토착민의 unity[júːnəti] 혱 단결, 협동

구문 1행 **Everyone** in the world **enjoys** the Olympic Games.
• everyone: every-로 시작하는 대명사는 단수 취급함

4행 …, thousands of people from over 40 tribes get together **to take part in** the games.
• to take part in: '…하기 위해서'의 의미로, 목적을 나타내는 부사적 용법의 to부정사구

13행 The highlight is a tree-log relay race, **where** runners run around with ….
• where: a tree-log relay race를 보충 설명하는 계속적 용법의 관계부사

18행 They **had** already **left** the stadium to enjoy a festival outside!
• had left: 과거 기준 시점까지의 동작의 완료를 나타내는 과거완료

STRATEGIC SUMMARY   similar, different, traditional, train, celebrate

EXPANDING KNOWLEDGE

1 *1)* ancient *2)* host *3)* disabled   **2** *1)* T *2)* F

어휘 ancient[éinʃənt] 혱 고대의 modern[mádərn] 혱 현대의 Paralympics[pærəlímpiks] 혱 (*pl.*) 세계

2

장애인 올림픽　disabled[diséibld] 형 장애를 가진　symbol[símbəl] 명 상징
presentation[prìːzentéiʃən] 명 제출; *수여, 증정　host[houst] 명 주최국, 주최측
committee[kəmíti] 명 위원회　[문제] properly[prɑ́pərli] 부 제대로　injury[índʒəri] 명 부상, 상처
consist of …로 구성되다

VOCABULARY REVIEW
A *1* archery *2* trunk *3* torch *4* celebrate
B *1* d *2* d　　**C** *1* c *2* b *3* d *4* a

unit *02* FOOD

pp. 12-15

★*The Croissant*

1 a　**2** c　**3** d　**4** Because the croissant as we know it today didn't appear in any books until 1906.　**5** d　**6** *1)* F *2)* T

프랑스에 가면, 많은 사람들이 초승달 모양의 페이스트리를 먹고 있는 것을 보게 될 것이다. 이 부드럽고, 바삭하고, 버터가 들어간 음식은 '크루아상'이라고 불리는데, 이는 프랑스어로 '초승달 모양'을 의미한다. 그것은 세계에서 가장 인기 있는 빵 종류 중 하나이다.

　그것의 이름이 프랑스어이기 때문에, 많은 사람들은 이것이 프랑스에서 유래된 것이라고 생각한다. 그러나 어떤 사람들은 그것이 사실 오스트리아에서 유래된 것이라고 말한다. 1683년에, 오스트리아는 터키와 전쟁 중이었다. 몇 달간의 공격 후에, 터키인들은 비엔나로 들어가기 위해 지하 터널을 파려고 했다. 때마침 지하에서 일하고 있던 몇몇 제빵사들이 땅을 파는 소리를 들었다. 제빵사들 덕분에, 오스트리아 군대는 터널을 파괴하고 적을 물리쳤다. 승리를 기념하기 위해, 제빵사들은 터키 국기에서 봤던 초승달 모양으로 페이스트리를 만들었다. 오스트리아인들이 그것들을 먹을 때, 그들은 터키인들을 베어 무는 것처럼 느꼈다!

　프랑스로 크루아상이 도입된 것에 관한 이야기도 있다. 루이 16세와 결혼한 오스트리아의 공주, 마리 앙투아네트가 약 100년 후에 프랑스로 크루아상을 들여왔다고 전해진다. 아마 그녀는 크루아상을 너무 좋아해서 그것 없이는 살 수 없었던 것일지도 모른다!

　그러나 오늘날 우리가 알고 있는 크루아상은 1906년까지 어떤 책에도 나오지 않았기 때문에 많은 사람들이 이 이야기들의 진실성을 의심한다. 그러나 비록 그것의 시작은 불분명할지라도, 크루아상이 오늘날 프랑스 문화의 상징이라는 것은 의심할 여지가 없다.

어휘　shaped[ʃeipt] 형 …의 모양의　pastry[péistri] 명 페이스트리　crispy[kríspi] 형 바삭바삭한
attack[ətǽk] 동 공격하다　dig[dig] 동 파다　underground[ʌ̀ndərgráund] 형 지하의
get into …에 들어가다　basement[béismənt] 명 지하　flag[flæg] 명 기, 깃발　bite[bait]
동 물다　doubt[daut] 동 의심하다 명 의심　appear[əpíər] 동 나타나다　uncertain[ʌnsə́ːrtn]
형 불분명한　[문제] army[ɑ́ːrmi] 명 군대　destroy[distrɔ́i] 동 파괴하다　defeat[difíːt]
동 패배시키다, 물리치다　enemy[énəmi] 명 적　introduction[ìntrədʌ́kʃən] 명 도입, 전래

구문　2행　This soft, crispy, buttery food is called a "croissant," **which** means "crescent" in French.
　　　• which: a "croissant"를 보충 설명하는 계속적 용법의 주격 관계대명사
　　　6행　..., the Turks tried to dig an underground tunnel **to get into** Vienna.
　　　• to get into: '…하기 위해'라는 의미로, 목적을 나타내는 부사적 용법의 to부정사구
　　　9행　..., the bakers made pastries in the shape of the crescent [**that** they *had seen* on the Turkish flag].

3

- that 이하는 the crescent를 수식하는 목적격 관계대명사절
- had seen: 주절의 시제보다 앞선 시점의 내용을 가리키는 과거완료

12행 **It** is said **that** *Marie Antoinette, the Austrian princess* [**who** married King Louis XVI], ….
- It은 가주어이고, that 이하가 진주어
- Marie Antoinette와 the Austrian princess는 동격
- who 이하는 the Austrian princess를 수식하는 주격 관계대명사절

14행 Maybe she liked croissants **too** much **to live** without them!
- too … to-v: 너무 …해서 ~할 수 없다

STRATEGIC SUMMARY discovered, destroy, victory, symbol

EXPANDING KNOWLEDGE

1 *1)* nutrient *2)* traditional *3)* flour   **2** *1)* T *2)* F

어휘 grain[grein] 똉 곡물 wheat[hwiːt] 똉 밀 rye[rai] 똉 호밀 oats[outs] 똉 (*pl.*) 귀리
ingredient[ingríːdiənt] 똉 재료, 성분 yeast[jiːst] 똉 이스트, 효모 nutrient[njúːtriənt]
똉 영양소, 영양분 carbohydrate[kàːrbouháidreit] 똉 탄수화물 dietary fiber 식이성 섬유
[문제] substance[sʌ́bstəns] 똉 물질 custom[kʌ́stəm] 똉 관습, 풍습 grind[graind] 똉 갈다

VOCABULARY REVIEW

A *1* dig *2* bite *3* attack *4* basement
B *1* c *2* b   **C** *1* a *2* d *3* b *4* b

unit 03 ORIGINS

pp. 16-19

★*Uncle Sam*

1 a **2** They began thinking of "Uncle Sam" as a nickname for the United States. **3** c **4** d **5** b
6 *1)* F *2)* T

미국 국기처럼 보이는 정장 모자와 옷을 착용한 키가 큰 남자를 본 적이 있는가? 그는 유명한 미국의 아이콘인 Uncle Sam이다. 그러면 그는 어디에서 유래했는가?

1812년 전쟁 중에, Sam이라는 이름의 정육업자는 미국 육군에 고기를 공급했다. 그가 보낸 통에는 미국을 나타내는 U.S.가 적혀 있었다. 하지만 군인들은 그 글자들이 Uncle Sam을 뜻한다고 농담을 했다. 사람들이 이 이야기를 듣고, 'Uncle Sam'을 미국의 별명으로 생각하기 시작했다.

Uncle Sam의 첫 이미지는 1830년대에 한 정치 만화에 등장했다. 하지만 그는 오늘날의 그와 같이 보이지 않았다. 그가 처음 등장한 후에, 그의 이미지는 그림마다 바뀌었다. 남북 전쟁 무렵, Uncle Sam은 에이브러햄 링컨 대통령을 닮게 그려졌다. 그래서, 그는 턱수염이 있는 키가 크고, 마른 남자가 되었다. 또한, 그는 보통 성조기 무늬의 정장을 입고 정장 모자를 쓰고 있었다. 그러나 Uncle Sam의 가장 유명한 이미지는 1차 세계 대전의 모병 포스터에 나온 것이다. 이 포스터에서, 그는 그의 아래에 쓰인 '나는 미국 육군을 위해 당신을 원합니다'라는 문구와 함께, 보는 사람을 응시하며 손가락으로 가리키고 있다. 이 그림은 그를 유명한 국가적 상징으로 만들었다.

오늘날, Uncle Sam의 이 이미지는 미국의 대중문화에서 종종 사용된다. 예를 들어, 유명한 야구팀인 뉴욕 양키스는 Uncle Sam의 모자를 그들의 팀 로고에 사용한다.

어휘 top hat 서양의 남성 정장용 모자 icon[áikan] 똉 우상, 아이콘 meatpacker[míːtpæ̀kər]

4

명 정육업자   barrel[bǽrəl] 명 (목재·금속으로 된 대형) 통   mark[ma:rk] 동 (이름·표시 등을)
…에 적다   stand for …을 나타내다   nickname[níknèim] 명 별명   political[pəlítikəl]
형 정치적인   cartoon[ka:rtú:n] 명 만화   appearance[əpíərəns] 명 외모; *등장, 출현
beard[biərd] 명 턱수염   recruit[rikrú:t] 동 (신병 등을) 모집하다   stare[stɛər] 동 응시하다
point[pɔint] 동 가리키다   phrase[freiz] 명 문구   beneath[biní:θ] 전 아래에   popular culture
대중문화   logo[lóugou] 명 로고, 상징   [문제] resemble[rizémbl] 동 닮다   president[prézədənt]
명 대통령

구문   1행   **Have** you ever **seen** a tall man in a top hat and clothes [*that* look like the
               American flag]?
                 • Have seen: '…한 적이 있다'의 의미로, 경험을 나타내는 현재완료
                 • that 이하는 a top hat and clothes를 수식하는 주격 관계대명사절
        5행   …, a meatpacker [**named** Sam] *provided* the U.S. Army *with* meat.
                 • named 이하는 a meatpacker를 수식하는 과거분사구
                 • provide A with B: A에게 B를 공급하다
        7행   The barrels [(which[that]) **he sent**] were marked U.S., for the United States.
                 • he sent 앞에 The barrels를 선행사로 하는 목적격 관계대명사가 생략되어 있음
        11행   …, they began **thinking of** "Uncle Sam" **as** a nickname for the United States.
                 • think of A as B: A를 B로 생각하다[여기다]
        22행   This picture **made** him **a well-known national symbol**.
                 • make + 목적어 + 명사: …을 ~로 만들다

STRATEGIC ORGANIZER   icon, provided, look like, popular

EXPANDING KNOWLEDGE

1 c   **2** 1) T   2) F

미국에 Uncle Sam이 있는 것처럼, 영국에는 국가의 상징으로 John Bull이 있다. John Bull은 18세기 J. Arbuthnot이 쓴 책 시리즈에 나오는 인물이었다. 그 책들은 그를 영국을 대표하는 정직하고 마음씨가 좋은 남자로 묘사했다. 그가 인기를 얻게 되자, 정치 풍자 만화가들은 그를 자신들의 작품에 그리기 시작했다. 그는 보통 옆에 불도그와 함께 있는 뚱뚱한 남자로 그려졌다. 그는 또한 정장을 입고, 정장 모자를 쓰고, 영국 국기처럼 보이는 조끼를 입었다. 그는 책과 연극 속에, 그리고 심지어 상표명으로도 자주 등장했다! 그러나 1950년대 이후로, 그는 덜 자주 보였다. 그럼에도 불구하고, 영국 사람들은 여전히 그에게 큰 애정을 가지고 있다!

어휘   character[kǽriktər] 명 등장인물   goodhearted[gúdhá:rtid] 형 친절한, 마음씨가 고운
         represent[rèprizént] 동 대표하다   cartoonist[ka:rtú:nist] 명 만화가   waistcoat[wéskət] 명 조끼
         nevertheless[nèvərðəlés] 부 그럼에도 불구하고

구문   3행   The books **described** him **as** an honest, goodhearted man [*representing* Britain].
                 • describe A as B: A를 B로 묘사하다
                 • representing 이하는 an honest, goodhearted man을 수식하는 현재분사구
        7행   …, and a waistcoat [**that** looked like the Union Jack].
                 • that 이하는 a waistcoat를 수식하는 주격 관계대명사절

VOCABULARY REVIEW

A   **1** mark   **2** logo   **3** phrase   **4** recruit
B   **1** c   **2** b   **C**   **1** d   **2** b   **3** c   **4** b

★*Differences in Shopping Behavior*

1 c **2** c **3** c **4** b **5** c **6** 1) F 2) T

'남자는 그가 필요한 1달러짜리 물건에 대해 2달러를 지불할 것이다. 여자는 그녀가 필요하지 않은 2달러짜리 물건에 대해 1달러를 지불할 것이다.' 이것은 현실에 딱 맞는 농담이다. 쇼핑에 관한 한, 남자와 여자는 서로 다른 행성 사람들이다.

남자와 여자가 쇼핑몰에서 청바지를 어떻게 사는지 생각해보라. 남자들은 보통 바로 청바지 가게로 걸어가서 최저 가격을 알아보지도 않고, 즉시 바지를 산다. 하지만, 여자들은 보통 쇼핑몰을 먼저 돌아다닌 후에 청바지를 산다. 그들은 필요하지 않은 갖가지 다른 물건들의 할인가를 살펴보고, 향수를 테스트해보는 일과 같은 다른 일들을 하기 위해 멈춰 선다.

그렇다면 왜 남자와 여자는 이렇게 다르게 쇼핑을 하는 것일까? 어떤 학자들은 이것이 남자와 여자가 생각하는 방식에서의 차이 때문이라고 생각한다. 남자들은 보통 쇼핑을 완수해야 할 임무라고 생각해서, 그것을 빨리해버리려고 노력한다. 반대로, 여자들은 쇼핑을 오락이라고 생각하고 쇼핑하며 돌아다니는 데 시간을 보내는 것을 좋아한다.

물론, 이러한 차이가 옳고 그름의 문제는 아니다. 그러나 이런 서로 다른 사고방식을 아는 것은 남자와 여자가 쇼핑몰에서 함께 즐기는 데 도움이 될 수 있다. 예를 들면, 요즘 많은 백화점에 남성 휴게실이 있는데, 그곳에서 남자들은 아내가 쇼핑을 하는 동안 스포츠를 볼 수 있다.

어휘 item[áitəm] 뗑 물품, 품목   true[tru:] 혱 사실의; *…에 적용되는[해당하는]   reality[riǽləti] 뗑 현실   when it comes to …에 관한 한   planet[plǽnit] 뗑 행성   mall[mɔːl] 뗑 쇼핑몰 directly[diréktli] 뛰 곧장   search for …을 찾다   best price 최저 가격   check out 확인하다; *살펴보다   discount[dískaunt] 뗑 할인   a variety of 다양한, 여러 가지의   perfume[pə́ːrfjuːm] 뗑 향수   scholar[skálər] 뗑 학자   mission[míʃən] 뗑 임무   complete[kəmplíːt] 동 완료하다, 끝마치다   recreational[rèkriéiʃənəl] 혱 오락의   matter[mǽtər] 뗑 문제   lounge[launʤ] 뗑 휴게실, 라운지   [문제] gender[ʤéndər] 뗑 성, 성별   must-have[mʌ́sthǽv] 혱 꼭 필요한, 반드시 가져야 하는   wander[wándər] 동 거닐다

구문 1행 A man will pay $2 for a $1 item [(which[that]) **he needs**].
• he needs 앞에 a $1 item을 선행사로 하는 목적격 관계대명사가 생략되어 있음

6행 Think about [**how** men and women shop for jeans at the mall].
• how 이하는 '의문사 + 주어 + 동사' 어순의 간접의문문으로, 전치사 about의 목적어 역할을 함

15행 Men usually **think of** shopping **as** a mission *to complete*, ...
• think of A as B: A를 B라고 생각하다[여기다]
• to complete: a mission을 수식하는 형용사적 용법의 to부정사

17행 On the contrary, women **find** it **recreational** and ....
• find + 목적어 + 목적격보어(형용사): …을 ~라고 여기다

21행 However, [**knowing** these different ways of thinking] can *help* men and women *have* fun together ....
• knowing 이하는 문장의 주어로 쓰인 동명사구
• help + 목적어 + 동사원형: …가 ~하도록 돕다

26행 ... have a men's lounge, **where** men can watch sports ....
• where: a men's lounge를 보충 설명하는 계속적 용법의 관계부사

STRATEGIC ORGANIZER quickly, mission, pastime, fun

EXPANDING KNOWLEDGE

1 spouse **2** feminine **3** equality **4** discrimination

어휘   male[meil] 명 남자   female[fíːmeil] 명 여자   masculine[mǽskjulin] 형 남성의
feminine[fémənin] 형 여성의   individual[ìndəvídʒuəl] 형 개인의   race[reis] 명 인종
mate[meit] 명 친구, 짝   spouse[spaus] 명 배우자   population[pàpjuléiʃən] 명 인구
equality[ikwάləti] 명 평등   identity[aidéntəti] 명 정체   discrimination[diskrìmənéiʃən] 명 차별
stereotype[stériətàip] 명 고정 관념   [문제] quality[kwάləti] 명 특징, 특성   associated with …와
관련된   unfair[ʌnféər] 형 부당한, 불공평한   treatment[tríːtmənt] 명 대우

VOCABULARY REVIEW

A   **1** mission   **2** scholar   **3** lounge   **4** recreational
B   **1** b   **2** d   **C**   **1** c   **2** d   **3** b   **4** d

unit 05 LITERATURE

pp. 24-27

★ *William Tell*

1 b   **2** d   **3** c   **4** c   **5** b   **6** d

> 오래전, 스위스는 게슬러라는 이름의 잔혹한 남자에 의해 통치되고 있었다. 어느 날, 그는 긴 장대 꼭대기에 자신의 모자를 놓고 백성들에게 그것에 절을 하라고 명령했다. 그러나 …
>
> 윌리엄 텔이라는 남자는 절하기를 거부했다. 게슬러는 매우 화가 나서 그를 벌할 잔인한 계획을 생각해냈다. 게슬러는 윌리엄 텔이 사냥꾼이고 석궁을 아주 잘 쏜다는 것을 알고 있었다. 그래서 그는 병사들에게 텔의 어린 아들을 머리 위에 사과를 얹은 채로 세워 놓도록 명령했다. 그러고 나서 그는 윌리엄 텔에게 화살로 그 사과를 쏘라고 명령했다. 게슬러는 그에게 "만약 네가 하지 않으면, 내 병사들이 네 아들을 죽일 것이다."라고 말했다.
>
>   윌리엄 텔은 그것을 하기를 주저했다. "제 아들이 움직이면 어찌합니까? 화살이 사과를 빗나간다면 어찌합니까?"라고 그가 물었다. 그리고 그는 "제발! 이것을 하지 않게 해주시오."라고 간청했다. 그러나 게슬러는 그를 무시했다. 하지만 윌리엄 텔의 아들은 두려워하지 않았다. 그는 아버지가 자신의 머리 위에서 사과를 쉽게 쏘아 떨어뜨릴 만큼 충분히 실력이 있다는 믿음이 있었다. 윌리엄 텔은 조용히 석궁과 두 개의 화살을 집어 들고, 신중하게 겨냥을 했다.
>
>   윙– 그의 화살은 허공을 가르고 날아가 사과의 중앙을 맞혔고, 아들의 머리 위에서 그것을 떨어뜨렸다! 모여 있던 마을 사람들은 기뻐서 환호했다! 게슬러는 화가 났고, 그때 다른 화살을 보았다. "왜 너는 두 개의 화살을 집어 들었느냐?"라고 그가 윌리엄 텔에게 물었다. "만약 내 아이가 다쳤다면, 나는 두 번째 화살로 당신의 심장을 쏘았을 것이오."라고 텔은 침착하게 대답했다.

어휘   rule[ruːl] 동 통치하다   cruel[krúːəl] 형 잔혹한, 무자비한   place[pleis] 동 두다, 놓다
pole[poul] 명 막대기, 장대   bow[bau] 동 절하다   punish[pʌ́niʃ] 동 벌하다
crossbow[krɔ́ːsbòu] 명 석궁   shoot[ʃuːt] 동 쏘다   arrow[ǽrou] 명 화살   hesitant[hézətənt]
형 주저하는   beg[beg] 동 간청하다   ignore[ignɔ́ːr] 동 무시하다   faith[feiθ] 명 믿음
skilled[skild] 형 숙련된, 노련한   aim[eim] 명 목표; *겨냥, 조준   whiz[hwiz] 명 윙(화살이 내는 소리)
cheer[tʃiər] 동 환호하다   calmly[kάːmli] 부 침착하게   [문제] bravery[bréivəri] 명 용기
arrest[ərést] 동 체포하다   evil[íːvəl] 형 사악한   moral[mɔ́ːrəl] 형 도덕적인   wicked[wíkid]
형 못된, 사악한   mean[miːn] 형 못된, 심술궂은   intend[inténd] 동 의도하다

9행 So he **ordered** his soldiers **to** *make* Tell's young son *stand* with an apple ....
- order + 목적어 + to-v: …에게 ~하라고 명령하다
- 사역동사(make) + 목적어 + 동사원형: …가 ~하게 하다

17행 **What if** my son should move?
- what if: '…하면 어떻게 될까?'의 의미로, if 뒤에 가정법이 쓰임(= what would happen if)

20행 He had faith [**that** his father was skilled *enough to* easily *shoot* the apple off his head].
- that: faith와 동격인 명사절을 이끄는 접속사
- enough to-v: …할 정도로 충분히

25행 … struck the center of the apple, [**knocking** it off his son's head]!
- knocking 이하는 연속동작을 나타내는 분사구문

29행 …, "If my child **had been harmed**, I **would have shot** the second one through your heart."
- if + 주어 + had v-ed, 주어 + 조동사의 과거형 + have v-ed: 가정법 과거완료

STRATEGIC SUMMARY   refused, punish, hesitated, succeeded

EXPANDING KNOWLEDGE

1 behavior   **2** attempt   **3** curious   **4** honest

어휘   courage[kə́ːridʒ] 명 용기 (courageous 형 용감한)   challenge[tʃǽlindʒ] 명 도전
curious[kjúəriəs] 형 호기심 많은   generous[dʒénərəs] 형 너그러운   heroic[hiróuik] 형 영웅다운
fearless[fíərlis] 형 두려움을 모르는   adventurous[ædvéntʃərəs] 형 모험심이 강한
shy[ʃai] 형 수줍음을 많이 타는   timid[tímid] 형 소심한   cowardly[káuərdli] 형 겁이 많은
spirit[spírit] 명 정신, 영혼; *(특정한 유형의) 사람   attempt[ətémpt] 명 시도
behavior[bihéivjər] 명 행동   put on a brave face 자신 있는 척하다   [문제] cheat[tʃiːt] 동 속이다

VOCABULARY REVIEW

A   **1** rule   **2** timid   **3** ignore   **4** beg
B   **1** b   **2** c   **C**   **1** c   **2** b   **3** d   **4** c

unit **06 MUSIC**

pp. 28-31

★*Antonio Salieri*

1 d   **2** a   **3** c   **4** b   **5** he[Salieri] was just a jealous, common composer who murdered Mozart
6 c

> 당신은 누가 위대한 작곡가인 베토벤, 슈베르트, 그리고 리스트를 가르쳤는지 아는가? 그들의 스승은 이름이 안토니오 살리에리인 뛰어난 작곡가였다.
>
> 그는 당신에게 익숙하지 않을지도 모르지만, 그는 일생 동안 유럽에서 유명한 음악가였다. 그는 이십 대였을 때 오스트리아 황제에 의해 고용되었다. 그리고 그는 38년 동안 궁정의 수석 작곡가로 일했다. 그 시기 동안, 그는 훌륭한 오페라와 교회 음악, 그리고 다른 고전 음악들을 작곡했다.
>
> 하지만 살리에리가 그렇게 대단했다면, 왜 그는 오늘날 유명하지 않은 것인가? 그것은 모차르트와 관련된 소문 때문이다. 살리에리는 아주 성공했지만, 사람들은 모차르트가 살리에리는 가지지 못한 음악적 천재성을 가지고 있다고

생각했다. (음악에서 성공하기 위해서는, 노력이 천재성보다 더 중요하다.) 이 때문에, 많은 사람들이 살리에리가 모차르트를 시기했다고 믿었다. 그래서, 모차르트가 갑자기 죽었을 때, 살리에리가 그에게 독약을 주었다는 소문이 생겨났다.

　　그 이후로, 사람들은 그의 음악 작품보다 이 소문에 더 집중해왔다. 게다가, 오페라와 연극, 그리고 영화가 이 이야기를 전한다. 그것들은 사람들로 하여금 살리에리가 모차르트를 살해한 그저 시기심 많고, 평범한 작곡가라고 생각하게 한다.

　　그러나 새로운 연구들이 모차르트가 자연사했다는 것을 보여줌에 따라, 많은 사람들이 살리에리와 그의 작품에 대해 더 많은 관심을 보이고 있다. 그리고 이탈리아에는 그의 음악을 기념하는 연례 축제까지 있다!

어휘 composer[kəmpóuzər] 명 작곡가　brilliant[bríljənt] 형 뛰어난　lifetime[láiftàim] 명 일생, 생애
hire[haiər] 동 고용하다　emperor[émpərər] 명 황제　royal[rɔ́iəl] 형 국왕의　court[kɔːrt]
명 법정; *궁궐　chief[tʃiːf] 형 (계급 · 직급상) 최고의　classical[klǽsikəl] 형 고전적인; *(음악이)
클래식의　rumor[rúːmər] 명 소문　genius[dʒíːnjəs] 명 천재성　jealous[dʒéləs] 형 시기하는;
질투심 많은　poison[pɔ́izn] 명 독약 동 독살하다　common[kámən] 형 흔한; *평범한
murder[mə́ːrdər] 동 살해하다 (murderer 명 살인자)　die of …로 죽다　natural cause 자연적
원인　annual[ǽnjuəl] 형 매년의, 연례의　[문제] myth[miθ] 명 신화; *(근거 없는) 이야기
compare A with B A를 B와 비교하다　influence[ínfluəns] 동 영향을 미치다

구문 1행　Do you know [**who** taught the great composers Beethoven, Schubert, and Liszt]?
　　　　• who 이하는 '의문사(주어) + 동사' 어순의 간접의문문으로, 동사 know의 목적어 역할을 함
　　　2행　Their teacher was a brilliant composer [**whose** name was Antonio Salieri].
　　　　• whose 이하는 a brilliant composer를 수식하는 소유격 관계대명사절
　　　12행　…, but people thought Mozart had a musical genius [**that** Salieri didn't have].
　　　　• that 이하는 a musical genius를 수식하는 목적격 관계대명사절
　　　16행　…, the rumor was born [**that** Salieri *had given* him poison].
　　　　• that: the rumor와 동격인 명사절을 이끄는 접속사
　　　　• had given: 주절의 시제보다 앞선 시점의 내용을 가리키는 과거완료
　　　19행　They **make** people **think** Salieri was just a jealous, common composer [*who murdered Mozart*].
　　　　• 사역동사(make) + 목적어 + 동사원형: …가 ~하게 하다
　　　　• who 이하는 a jealous, common composer를 수식하는 주격 관계대명사절

STRATEGIC SUMMARY　classical, jealous, naturally, interested

EXPANDING KNOWLEDGE

1　*1)* contemporary　*2)* medieval　*3)* percussion　　**2**　*1)* T　*2)* F

어휘　period[píːəriəd] 명 기간; 시대　medieval[mìːdíːvəl] 형 중세의　practice[prǽktis] 명 관습
era[íərə] 명 시대　contemporary[kəntémpərèri] 형 동시대의; *현대의
instrument[ínstrəmənt] 명 악기　string[striŋ] 명 현악기　woodwind[wúdwìnd] 명 목관악기
brass[bræs] 명 금관악기　percussion[pərkʌ́ʃən] 명 타악기

VOCABULARY REVIEW

A　**1** chief　**2** composer　**3** genius　**4** poison
B　**1** c　**2** b　　**C**　**1** c　**2** c　**3** b　**4** a

07 SCIENCE

pp. 32-35

★Doctors' Green Gowns

1 d **2** Looking at the green color of their gown (during surgery) does. **3** *1)* c *2)* b *3)* a
4 b **5** c **6** d

> **Q:** 의사들은 보통 흰 상의를 입습니다. 그런데 왜 수술할 때는 항상 초록색 가운을 입나요?
>
> **A:** 수술할 때 입는 가운의 색깔은 여러 가지 이유로 신중히 선정되었습니다. 가장 중요하게는, 초록색은 눈이 편안해지도록 돕습니다. 선홍색 피를 오랫동안 응시한 후에, 의사의 눈은 피로해질 수 있습니다. 하지만 수술하는 동안 가운의 초록색을 응시하는 것이 그들의 눈이 나아지도록 해줍니다.
>
> 또 다른 이유는 '잔상'과 관련이 있습니다. 사람들이 한 색상을 너무 오래 응시하면, 그것은 그들 눈의 어떤 세포를 피곤하게 합니다. 그러고 나서, 그들이 흰 바탕을 바라보면, 반대색의 떠 있는 형체인 잔상을 보게 됩니다. 그래서 의사들이 흰색 가운을 입었을 때, 그들은 가운에서 붉은색의 반대색인 초록색 잔상을 보았습니다. 하지만 이 문제는 초록색 가운을 입음으로써 쉽게 해결되었습니다. (하지만 일부 의사들은 여전히 초록색 가운 대신에 흰색 가운을 입는 것을 좋아합니다.) 이는 가운의 초록색이 붉은 피의 잔상을 막아주기 때문입니다. 결과적으로, 의사들은 수술에 더 잘 집중할 수 있습니다.
>
> 게다가, 수술 중에 초록색 옷을 입는 것은 핏자국을 감추도록 돕습니다. 붉은색 피는 흰옷에서 눈에 잘 띕니다. 하지만 초록색 옷에서, 피는 갈색으로 변하고, 심지어는 그것을 거의 알아볼 수도 없습니다. 그러므로 의사들이 초록색 가운을 입는 세 가지 타당한 이유가 있습니다!

어휘 coat[kout] 圐 외투; *상의   gown[gaun] 圐 (여성의) 드레스; *(의사 등이 입는) 가운
perform[pərfɔ́ːrm] 圐 행하다, 수행하다   surgery[sə́ːrdʒəri] 圐 수술   stare at …을 빤히 쳐다보다, 응시하다   be related to …와 관계가 있다   afterimage[ǽftərìmidʒ] 圐 잔상   certain[sə́ːrtn] 圐 확실한; *어떤   cell[sel] 圐 세포   background[bǽkgràund] 圐 배경   floating[flóutiŋ] 圐 떠 있는   shape[ʃeip] 圐 모양, 형태   opposite[ápəzit] 圐 반대의 圐 반대(되는 것)   prevent[privént] 圐 막다, 방지하다   concentrate on …에 집중하다   stain[stein] 圐 얼룩   stand out 쉽게 눈에 띄다

구문 6행 But [**looking** at the green color of their gown during surgery] *makes* their eyes *feel* better.
　　　　　• looking 이하는 문장의 주어로 쓰인 동명사구
　　　　　• 사역동사(make) + 목적어 + 동사원형: …가 ~하게 하다
　　　9행 …, it **causes** certain cells in their eyes **to become** tired.
　　　　　• cause + 목적어 + to-v: …가 ~하게 하다
　　　12행 …, they saw afterimages [**that** were green, the opposite color of red], ….
　　　　　• that 이하는 afterimages를 수식하는 주격 관계대명사절
　　　21행 So there are three good reasons [**why** doctors wear green gowns]!
　　　　　• why 이하는 three good reasons를 수식하는 관계부사절

STRATEGIC ORGANIZER relaxes, prevent, hide, noticeable

EXPANDING KNOWLEDGE

1 illusion **2** normal **3** inspire **4** sense

어휘 vision[víʒən] 圐 시력; 환상, 상상   view[vjuː] 圐 견해; 시야   sight[sait] 圐 시력; 광경

visible[vízəbl] 형 보이는, 알아볼 수 있는   visual[víʒuəl] 형 시각의   inspire[inspáiər] 동 고무하다, 격려하다   illusion[ilúːʒən] 명 환상   normal[nɔ́ːrməl] 형 보통의, 정상적인   20-20 vision 완벽한[정상] 시력   [문제] ordinary[ɔ́ːrdənèri] 형 보통의, 일상적인

VOCABULARY REVIEW

A **1** perform   **2** relax   **3** cell   **4** afterimage
B **1** c **2** a   C **1** d **2** c **3** b **4** b

★Coffeehouses: More than Drinking Coffee

1 d   **2** Because they thought it inspired creativity and provided energy.   **3** b   **4** d   **5** c
6 b

> 요즘, 커피숍은 어디에서나 찾아볼 수 있다. 하지만 그 인기는 새로운 것이 아니다. 17세기와 18세기 영국에서, 커피숍은 오늘날만큼이나 인기가 있었다.
>
> 커피는 영국에 16세기에 처음으로 전해졌다. 커피가 영국에 들어오기 전에, 사람들은 주로 맥주와 포도주를 마셨다. 하지만 사람들이 커피를 건강 음료라고 생각했기 때문에 커피는 곧 인기를 얻게 되었다. 그들은 커피가 창의력을 불러일으키고 활력을 준다고 생각했다. 1650년에, 첫 번째 영국 커피숍이 옥스퍼드에서 문을 열었다. (그러나 다른 지역에서는, 커피숍이 인기가 없었다.) 곧 커피숍은 전국에 퍼지기 시작했다. 불과 25년 후, 영국 전역에는 3,000개가 넘는 커피숍이 있었다.
>
> 커피의 인기가 커피숍 확산의 유일한 이유는 아니었다. 그 당시, 커피숍은 인기 있는 <u>사회 교류 장소</u>였다. 사람들은 커피를 마시거나, 그날의 소식들을 듣거나, 다양한 배경의 사람들을 만나기 위해 커피숍에 갔다. 그들은 또한 정치와 철학에서부터 과학과 사업에 이르는 다양한 주제들을 토론했다. 게다가, 단 1페니만으로, 사람들은 커피 한 잔을 살 수 있었을 뿐만 아니라, 읽을 신문이나 책을 빌릴 수도 있었다. <u>그 결과</u>, 이러한 커피숍들은 '페니 대학'이라고 불렸다.
>
> 이 모든 것이 17세기와 18세기 영국에서 커피숍을 주요한 지적 중심지로 만들었다.

어휘   popularity[pàpjulǽrəti] 명 인기 (unpopular 형 인기 없는)   introduce[ìntrədjúːs] 동 소개하다; *(처음으로) 전하다[들여오다]   inspire[inspáiər] 동 격려하다; *불어넣다, 고취시키다
creativity[krìːeitívəti] 명 창의력, 창조력   provide[prəváid] 동 공급하다, 주다   region[ríːdʒən] 명 지방, 지역   spread[spred] 동 퍼지다 확산, 전파   throughout[θruːáut] 전 …의 도처에
discuss[diskʌ́s] 동 논의하다, 토론하다   topic[tápik] 명 화제, 주제   politics[pálətiks] 명 정치
philosophy[filásəfi] 명 철학   intellectual[ìntəléktʃuəl] 형 지적인   [문제] long-lasting
[lɔ́ːŋlǽstiŋ] 형 오래 지속되는   youth[juːθ] 명 젊은이   institution[ìnstətjúːʃən] 명 기관, 단체
social[sóuʃəl] 형 사회적인   interaction[ìntərǽkʃən] 명 상호작용

구문   2행   However, their popularity is **nothing new**.
             • nothing new: -thing으로 끝나는 대명사는 형용사가 뒤에서 수식함
       4행   ..., coffee shops were just **as popular as** they are today.
             • as + 형용사의 원급 + as: …만큼 ~한
       9행   However, coffee soon became popular because people **considered** it **to be** a healthy drink.
             • consider + 목적어 + 목적격보어(to-v): …을 ~라고 생각하다
       21행 They also discussed a variety of topics [*ranging from* politics and philosophy *to* science and business].

11

- ranging 이하는 a variety of topics를 수식하는 현재분사구
- range from A to B: (범위가) A부터 B까지 이르다

24행 …, people could **not only** buy a cup of coffee **but also** borrow a newspaper ….
- not only A but also B: A뿐만 아니라 B도

STRATEGIC SUMMARY popular, healthy, discuss, universities

EXPANDING KNOWLEDGE

1 *1)* rich *2)* social *3)* cultivation   **2** *1)* T *2)* F

어휘 cultivation[kʌltəvéiʃən] 뗑 경작, 재배   in order 순으로, 순서대로   process[práses] 뗑 과정
roast[roust] 통 볶다   grind[graind] 통 갈다   brew[bru:] 통 끓이다   benefit[bénəfit] 뗑 이점
improvement[imprú:vmənt] 뗑 향상   rich[ritʃ] 휑 부유한; *…이 풍부한
antioxidant[æntiάksidənt] 뗑 산화 방지제   risk[risk] 뗑 위험   blood pressure 혈압
dehydration[dì:haidréiʃən] 뗑 탈수; *탈수증   fair trade 공정 거래

VOCABULARY REVIEW

A *1* unpopular *2* spread *3* topic *4* philosophy
B *1* b *2* a   **C** *1* a *2* c *3* c *4* d

unit 09 FESTIVALS   pp. 40-43

★ *The Holi Festival in India*

1 b **2** a **3** d **4** Because (he got angry that) his son worshipped a god instead of him. **5** a
6 c

사람들이 서로에게 빨간 가루를 던지고 있다. 어떤 사람들은 심지어 모르는 사람들에게 노란 물로 가득 찬 풍선을 던지고 있다. 물총을 가진 아이들 또한 서로에게 물을 뿌리고 있다. 하지만 놀랍게도, 아무도 화를 내지 않는다. 오히려, 모두가 기뻐 보인다. 무슨 일이 일어나고 있는 것일까? 이 사람들은 인도에서 가장 흥미로운 축제 중 하나인 Holi를 축하하고 있다!

Holi는 매년 3월 보름 다음 날에 거행된다. 그것은 봄을 맞이하고 풍작을 기원하기 위해 열린다. 축제 동안, 사람들은 꽃과 채소로 만들어진 형형색색의 가루로 스스로를 장식한다. 각각의 색은 고유한 의미를 가진다. 예를 들어, 빨간색은 활력을 나타내고 녹색은 조화를 의미한다.

Holi는 또한 Hiranyakasipu 왕의 여동생인 Holika의 이야기와 관련이 있다. 그 왕은 자신이 신들보다 더 위대하다고 믿었다. 그래서 아들인 Prahlad가 자신 대신에 한 신을 숭배하자, 왕은 화가 나서 Holika에게 Prahlad를 죽이라고 명령했다. 이 사악한 여자는 자신의 어린 조카를 불에 태워 죽이려고 했으나, 그녀의 계획은 실패했다. 결국, 그녀는 Prahlad 대신 불에 타 죽었다. 이것을 기념하기 위해, 사람들은 축제 전날 밤 커다란 모닥불을 피운다.

오늘날, 인도 사람들뿐만 아니라 전 세계에서 온 관광객들도 Holi를 즐긴다. 축제에 참가한 사람들은 결국 여러 색깔로 뒤덮이게 되는데, 이는 마치 그들이 하나의 큰 팔레트인 것처럼 모두를 화합시켜준다!

어휘 powder[páudər] 뗑 가루   stranger[stréindʒər] 뗑 낯선[모르는] 사람   pistol[pístəl] 뗑 총
spray[sprei] 통 뿌리다   festival[féstəvəl] 뗑 축제   harvest[hά:rvist] 뗑 수확, 추수
decorate[dékərèit] 통 장식하다, 꾸미다   colorful[kʌ́lərfəl] 휑 형형색색의, 다채로운
unique[ju:ní:k] 휑 독특한; *고유한   represent[rèprizént] 통 나타내다
harmony[hά:rməni] 뗑 조화   worship[wə́:rʃip] 통 숭배하다   wicked[wíkid] 휑 사악한

bonfire[bánfàiər] 몡 모닥불   end up 결국 …하게 되다   unite[juːnáit] 통 결합하다, 통합하다

[문제] obey[oubéi] 통 복종하다   participate in …에 참여하다

구문   1행   Some are even throwing balloons [**filled** with yellow water] at strangers.
· filled 이하는 balloons를 수식하는 과거분사구

6행   It is held **to welcome** spring and **to pray** for a good harvest.
· to welcome과 to pray는 '…하기 위해'라는 의미로, 목적을 나타내는 부사적 용법의 to부정사

19행   People at the festival end up covered in various colors, **which** unites everyone *as if* they *were* one big color palette!
· which: 앞의 절을 선행사로 하는 계속적 용법의 주격 관계대명사
· as if + 가정법 과거: 마치 …인 것처럼

STRATEGIC ORGANIZER   colored, March, wicked, Enjoyed

EXPANDING KNOWLEDGE

1 *1)* religious *2)* entertainment *3)* literature   **2** *1)* T *2)* F

어휘   purpose[pə́ːrpəs] 몡 목적   celebration[sèləbréiʃən] 몡 기념 행사   entertainment[èntərtéinmənt]
몡 오락   feature[fíːtʃər] 몡 특징, 특색   firework[fáiərwə̀ːrk] 몡 *(pl.)* 불꽃놀이
beverage[bévəridʒ] 몡 음료   costume[kástjuːm] 몡 의상, 복장   religious[rilídʒəs] 혱 종교적인
literature[lítərətʃər] 몡 문학   seasonal[síːzənl] 혱 계절적인

VOCABULARY REVIEW

A **1** stranger **2** unite **3** pistol **4** worship
B **1** a **2** c   **C** **1** d **2** c **3** a **4** b

unit 10 PLACES
pp. 44-47

★ *The Orsay Museum*

1 d **2** c **3** Because modern, longer trains didn't fit on its short platforms. **4** d **5** c
6 *1)* F *2)* T

> 오르세 미술관은 파리에서 가장 유명한 명소 중의 하나이다. 그것은 루브르 미술관의 건너편인 센 강의 왼편 둑에 위치해 있다. 미술관은 르누아르, 모네, 그리고 반 고흐의 그림들을 포함해서, 많은 귀중한 예술품들을 소장하고 있다. (불행히도, 반 고흐는 권총으로 자살했다.) 미술관의 거의 모든 예술 작품들은 인상주의 시대인 1848년에서 1914년 사이에 프랑스에서 만들어졌다. 그래서 오르세는 세계에서 가장 큰 인상주의 미술관이다.
>
> 놀랍게도, 그 건물은 처음에 미술관이 아니었다. 사실, 그것은 기차역으로 건축되었다! 거의 40년 동안, 그것은 철도망의 일부였다. 그러나, 현대의 더 긴 기차들이 그것의 짧은 승강장에 맞지 않았기 때문에 그것은 결국 버려졌다.
>
> 1986년에, 그것은 회화와 조각, 사진의 방대한 수집품을 소장하는 미술관으로 다시 문을 열었다. 미술관 안의 예술품이 놀라울 뿐만 아니라, 미술관 건물 자체도 예술품이다. 그것이 기차역에서 개조되었기 때문에, 그 건물은 몇 가지 독특한 특징을 지닌다. 예를 들어, 거기에는 유리로 만들어진 높고 우아한 반구형 천장이 있는데, 이것은 많은 햇빛이 안으로 들어오게 한다. 이것은 방문객들이 예술품을 더 잘 볼 수 있게 해준다. 그것은 또한, 입구 근처에 거대하고 둥근 시계가 특징이다. 오늘날, 삼백만 명이 넘는 사람들이 매년 미술관을 방문한다.

어휘   attraction[ətrǽkʃən] 몡 명소, 명물   locate[lóukeit] 통 (특정 위치에) 두다, 설치하다
bank[bǽŋk] 몡 둑   priceless[práislis] 혱 값을 매길 수 없는, 귀중한   including[inklúːdiŋ] 전 …을

포함하여　impressionist[impréʃənist] 형 인상주의의 명 인상파 화가　period[píːəriəd] 명 기간; *시대
railroad[réilròud] 명 철도　eventually[ivéntʃuəli] 부 결과적으로　abandon[əbǽndən] 동 버리다
fit[fit] 동 맞다　platform[plǽtfɔːrm] 명 플랫폼, 승강장　house[hauz] 동 보관하다, 소장하다
collection[kəlékʃən] 명 수집품, 소장품　sculpture[skʌ́lptʃər] 명 조각(품)　convert[kənvə́ːrt]
동 전환하다, 개조하다　distinctive[distíŋktiv] 형 독특한　elegant[éligənt] 형 우아한
domed[doumd] 형 반구형의　ceiling[síːliŋ] 명 천장　view[vjuː] 동 보다　entrance[éntrəns]
명 입구　[문제] chest[tʃest] 명 가슴; *상자　former[fɔ́ːrmər] 형 이전의

구문	12행	In 1986, it reopened as a museum **to house** a huge collection of ….
		• to house: a museum을 수식하는 형용사적 용법의 to부정사
	13행	**Not only** *is the art* inside the museum amazing, **but** the museum building **itself** is a work of art.
		• not only A but (also) B: A뿐만 아니라 B도
		• is the art: 부정어(not only)가 문장 앞에 와서 주어와 동사가 도치됨
		• itself: the museum building을 강조하는 재귀대명사
	16행	…, it has a high, elegant, domed ceiling [**made** of glass], *which* lets lots of sunlight in.
		• made 이하는 a high, elegant, domed ceiling을 수식하는 과거분사구
		• which: 앞의 절을 선행사로 하는 계속적 용법의 주격 관계대명사

STRATEGIC ORGANIZER　bank, Impressionist, train station, ceiling

EXPANDING KNOWLEDGE

1　*1)* portrait　*2)* landscape　*3)* realism　　**2**　*1)* F　*2)* T

어휘　portrait[pɔ́ːrtrit] 명 초상화　landscape[lǽndskèip] 명 풍경화　still life 정물화
impressionism[impréʃənìzm] 명 인상주의　expressionism[ikspréʃənìzm] 명 표현주의
cubism[kjúːbizm] 명 입체파　realism[ríːəlìzm] 명 사실주의　metropolitan[mètrəpálitən]
형 대도시의

VOCABULARY REVIEW

A　**1** abandon　**2** distinctive　**3** create　**4** period
B　**1** b　**2** d　　**C**　**1** c　**2** b　**3** b　**4** d

★unit★ 11 ENTERTAINMENT pp. 48-51

★Video Games Live

1 a　**2** Because they use only short, simple sounds over and over.　**3** c　**4** b　**5** c　**6** *1)* T　*2)* F

비디오 게임 라이브는 인기 있는 비디오 게임에 나오는 음악이 연주되는 세계 순회 연주회이다. 비디오 게임 라이브가 로스앤젤레스에 왔을 때, 나는 그것을 놓칠 수 없었다. 그 오케스트라는 내가 가장 좋아하는 비디오 게임에 나오는 음악을 연주했다. 동시에, 게임 속 장면들이 거대한 스크린에 나와서, 연주회를 아주 인상적으로 만들었다!

　　노래들 중 일부는 퐁과 스페이스 인베이더스 같은 옛날 게임에서 나온 것이었다. 연주회 전에 나는 오케스트라가 그것들을 어떻게 연주할지 상상할 수 없었는데, 왜냐하면 그 노래들은 짧고 단순한 소리만 반복적으로 사용하기 때문이다. 그런데 그들은 이 게임들의 '삐-뿌'와 '던-던-던' 소리를 만들어내기 위해 드럼과 심벌즈 같은 악기를 솜씨 좋게 이용했다. 스타크래프트와 파이널 판타지 같은 더 최신 게임 노래들도 연주되었다. 그것들은 옛날 게임 음악보다

훨씬 더 웅장하고 더 복잡했다. 오케스트라가 그 노래들을 연주했을 때, 그것은 오히려 실제 클래식 음악 연주회에 가까웠다.

하지만 내가 가장 좋았던 부분은 비디오 게임 피아니스트인 Martin Leung의 연주였다. 그는 게임 노래의 메들리를 아름답게 연주했다. 그가 *슈퍼마리오 월드*의 노래를 원래 속도의 약 두 배로 연주했을 때 나는 매우 놀랐다. (게임을 할 때 음악의 속도가 매우 중요하다고 말해도 과언이 아니다.) 사람들은 그에게 가장 큰 소리로 환호했다.

음악 외에도, 여러 가지 다른 재미있는 것들이 있었다. 의상 경연 대회를 위해 게임 캐릭터로 분장한 사람들을 보는 것은 재미있었다. 그리고 레이저 쇼도 놀라웠다! 나는 모든 연령대의 사람들이 이 행사를 함께 즐기는 것을 볼 수 있어서 즐거웠다.

어휘　orchestra[ɔ́ːrkəstrə] 명 오케스트라, 관현악단　　perform[pərfɔ́ːrm] 동 연주하다
(performance 명 연주)　　at the same time 동시에　　giant[dʒáiənt] 형 거대한
dramatic[drəmǽtik] 형 극적인; *인상적인　　over and over 여러 번 되풀이하여　　cleverly[klévərli]
부 영리하게; *솜씨 좋게　　cymbal[símbəl] 명 (pl.) (악기) 심벌즈　　produce[prədjúːs] 동 만들어내다
grand[grænd] 형 웅장한　　complicated[kámpləkèitid] 형 복잡한　　classical[klǽsikəl] 형 고전적인;
*(음악이) 클래식의　　medley[médli] 명 메들리　　amazed[əméizd] 형 놀란 (amazing 형 놀라운)
original[ərídʒənl] 형 원래의　　cheer[tʃiər] 동 환호하다　　entertaining[èntərtéiniŋ] 형 재미있는,
즐거운　　dress up 분장시키다　　[문제] brand-new[brǽndnjúː] 형 아주 새로운, 신품의
repetitive[ripétətiv] 형 반복적인

구문
1행　Video Games Live is a world-touring concert [**where** music from popular video games is played].
　• where 이하는 a world-touring concert를 수식하는 관계부사절
4행　…, scenes from the games appeared on a giant screen, [**making** the concert very dramatic]!
　• making 이하는 연속동작을 나타내는 분사구문(= and they made)
7행　Before the concert, I couldn't imagine [**how** the orchestra would play them], ….
　• how 이하는 '의문사 + 주어 + 동사' 어순의 간접의문문으로, 동사 imagine의 목적어 역할을 함
23행　**It** was fun **to see** people [*dressed up* as game characters for the costume contest].
　• It은 가주어이고, to see 이하가 진주어
　• dressed up 이하는 people을 수식하는 과거분사구
26행　I was glad **to see** people of all ages *enjoying* this event together.
　• to see: 감정의 원인을 나타내는 부사적 용법의 to부정사
　• 지각동사(see) + 목적어 + v-ing: …가 ~하고 있는 것을 보다

STRATEGIC SUMMARY　orchestra, simple, classical, costume

EXPANDING KNOWLEDGE

1 audience　**2** impression　**3** broadcast　**4** exhibition

어휘　amusement[əmjúːzmənt] 명 재미, 오락　　exhibition[èksəbíʃən] 명 전시, 전시회
broadcast[brɔ́ːdkæst] 동 방송하다 명 방송　　impression[impréʃən] 명 인상, 느낌
audience[ɔ́ːdiəns] 명 청중, 관중; 관람객　　pleasing[plíːziŋ] 형 즐거운　　delightful[diláitfəl]
형 정말 기분 좋은　　fascinating[fǽsənèitiŋ] 형 매력적인; *아주 재미있는　　boring[bɔ́ːriŋ] 형 지루한
depressing[diprésiŋ] 형 우울한　　dull[dʌl] 형 따분한　　uninteresting[ʌníntərəstiŋ] 형 재미없는
[문제] artwork[áːrtwə̀ːrk] 명 예술품　　object[ábdʒikt] 명 물건, 물체

VOCABULARY REVIEW

A　**1** giant　**2** dramatic　**3** character　**4** orchestra
B　**1** b　**2** a　　　　C　**1** d　**2** c　**3** b　**4** c

★Dodo Birds

1 a **2** c **3** d **4** Because it wasn't afraid of people or other animals. **5** d **6** d

'도도새처럼 죽은'이라는 표현은 '완전히 죽은'이라는 의미이다. 도도새는 한때 모리셔스라는 아프리카의 섬에 살았다. 그러나 그 문구가 나타내는 것처럼, 그 종은 300년도 더 전에 사라졌다.

도도새가 멸종되기 전에, 그것의 서식지인 모리셔스 섬은 그 새에게는 낙원이었다. 그곳은 세상의 다른 곳으로부터 고립되어 있었고, 두려워할 적이 없었다. 또한, 그 새의 주식인 씨앗과 과일은 땅에서 쉽게 발견되었다. 이러한 환경 덕분에, 도도새는 날 필요가 없어서, 점차 닭처럼 땅에서 생활하는 새로 진화했다. 그것의 날개는 작아진 반면, 몸의 크기는 커졌다. 도도새는 약 1미터의 키에 몸무게가 23kg까지 나갔다.

1600년경에, 스페인과 포르투갈의 탐험가들이 그 새를 최초로 보았다. 그들은 '바보'라는 의미의 포르투갈 단어에 근거하여 그 새에게 도도라는 이름을 붙였다. 그들은 그 새가 사람들이나 다른 동물들을 두려워하지 않았기 때문에 바보 같다고 생각했다. 안타깝게도, 이것은 그 새를 배고픈 사냥꾼들의 쉬운 표적으로 만들었다. 탐험가들이 모리셔스 섬에 데려온 고양이와 개 같은 동물들 또한 그 새들을 잡아먹었다. 게다가, 사람들이 자신들의 집을 짓기 위해 숲을 파괴했기 때문에 도도새의 서식지가 사라졌다. 1681년에, 그들이 인간과 처음으로 마주친 후 100년도 안 되어, 마지막 도도새가 죽임을 당했다. 오늘날, 이 새에 대해 남아 있는 것이라고는 그것의 멸종에 대한 슬픈 이야기뿐이다.

어휘 expression[ikspréʃən] 몡 표현　completely[kəmplíːtli] 뷔 완전히　phrase[freiz] 몡 구, 구절
suggest[səgdʒést] 동 제안하다; *시사하다, 암시하다　species[spíːʃiːz] 몡 (생물의) 종
disappear[dìsəpíər] 동 사라지다 (disappearance 몡 사라짐)　extinct[ikstíŋkt] 혱 멸종된
paradise[pǽrədàis] 몡 천국; *낙원　isolated[áisəlèitid] 혱 외딴; *고립된　rest[rest] 몡 나머지
enemy[énəmi] 몡 적　seed[siːd] 몡 씨, 씨앗　gradually[grǽdʒuəli] 뷔 서서히
evolve[iválv] 동 발달하다; *진화하다　bound[baund] 혱 …에 발이 묶인
increase[inkríːs] 동 증가하다　weigh[wei] 동 무게가 …이다　explorer[iksplɔ́ːrər] 몡 탐험가
name[neim] 동 이름을 지어주다　habitat[hǽbitæt] 몡 서식지　destroy[distrɔ́i] 동 파괴하다
encounter[inkáuntər] 동 접하다, 마주치다　remain[riméin] 동 (없어지지 않고) 남다
[문제] fate[feit] 몡 운명　imaginary[imǽdʒənèri] 혱 가공의, 상상의
convenient[kənvíːnjənt] 혱 편리한　target[táːrgit] 몡 대상, 표적

구문 12행　They **named** it the dodo, (which was) *based on* the Portuguese word for "fool."
　　　　・name A B: A를 B라고 이름 짓다
　　　　・based on 앞에 '주격 관계대명사 + be동사'가 생략되어 있음
　　　14행　Unfortunately, this **made** it **an easy target** for hungry hunters.
　　　　・make + 목적어 + 명사: …을 ~로 만들다
　　　15행　Animals like cats and dogs [**that** the explorers brought to Mauritius] also ate the birds.
　　　　・that 이하는 Animals like cats and dogs를 수식하는 목적격 관계대명사절
　　　21행　Today, all [**that** remains of this bird] is the sad story of its disappearance.
　　　　・that: all을 선행사로 하는 주격 관계대명사로, all, no, little, much 등이 선행사로 올 때, 관계대명사는 주로 that이 사용됨

STRATEGIC SUMMARY extinct, evolved, explorers, destroyed

EXPANDING KNOWLEDGE

1 c **2** 1) F 2) T

슬프게도, 도도새가 멸종되었을 뿐만 아니라, 모리셔스 섬의 한 나무도 같은 운명에 직면할 위기에 처해 있다. 그것은 도도나무라고 불린다. 과학자들은 도도새가 멸종된 이후로 그 섬에 새로운 도도나무가 자라지 않았다는 것을 발견했다. 그들은 도도새가 도도나무의 씨앗이 자라도록 도왔다고 생각한다. 도도새는 그 씨앗을 먹을 때 그것의 단단한 껍질을 깨물었다. 그 씨앗은 나중에 변을 통해 도도새의 몸 밖으로 나와 자랄 수 있었다. 도도새 없이는, 새로운 나무들은 자랄 수 없었다! 하지만 다행히도, 과학자들은 칠면조도 그 씨앗들이 자라도록 도울 수 있다는 것을 발견했다. 그래서 바라건대 도도나무는 결국 '도도새처럼 죽게' 되지는 않을 것이다.

어휘   in danger of …할 위험이 있는   bite[bait] 통 물다, 베어 물다   tough[tʌf] 형 힘든; *단단한
shell[ʃel] 명 껍데기, 껍질   exit[égzit] 통 나가다   dropping[drápiŋ] 명 낙하; *(pl.) (동물의) 똥
fortunately[fɔ́ːrtʃənətli] 부 다행스럽게도   turkey[tə́ːrki] 명 칠면조   [문제] survive[sərváiv]
통 살아남다, 생존하다   affect[əfékt] 통 …에 영향을 미치다   ecosystem[íkousìstəm] 명 생태계
prevent[privént] 통 막다   extinction[ikstíŋkʃən] 명 멸종

구문   1행   Sadly, **not only** *is the dodo bird* extinct, **but** a tree on Mauritius ….
• not only A but (also) B: A뿐만 아니라 B도
• is the dodo bird: 부정어(not only)가 문장 앞에 와서 주어와 동사가 도치됨
2행   Scientists found that no new dodo trees **have grown** on the island *since* the dodo bird went extinct.
• have grown: '…해 왔다'라는 의미로, 계속을 나타내는 현재완료
• since: '…이후[부터] (지금까지)'라는 의미로, 주로 현재완료와 함께 쓰임

VOCABULARY REVIEW

A   **1** forest   **2** encounter   **3** evolve   **4** explorer
B   **1** d   **2** c   C   **1** b   **2** a   **3** b   **4** c

★unit★ 13 ARCHITECTURE   pp. 56-59

★ The Discomfort of Home

1 d   **2** d   **3** Because every light switch is in an unexpected place.   **4** d   **5** a   **6** *1)* F   *2)* T

집은 우리에게 큰 편안함을 준다. 그것이 집이 존재하는 이유이다! 하지만 예술가인 Shusaku Arakawa와 Madeline Gins는 집에 대해 색다르고 독특한 생각을 가지고 있었다. 그래서, 그들은 도쿄에 사람들의 인생을 바꿀 수 있는 아파트인, Reversible Destiny Lofts를 만들었다.

밖에서 보면, 이 아파트들은 구와 관, 그리고 정육면체로 이루어진 레고 블록들처럼 보인다. 더욱이, 각 부분은 패스트푸드 식당의 실내 놀이터처럼, 빨강, 오렌지, 분홍, 또는 파랑으로 칠해져 있다. 내부는 훨씬 더 놀랍다. 바닥은 평평하지 않고 초콜릿 칩 쿠키처럼 울퉁불퉁하다. 부엌에는 갑자기 푹 꺼지는 바닥이 있다. 모든 조명 스위치는 예상치 못한 장소에 있어서, 불을 켜려면 주위를 더듬거려야 한다. 또한, 베란다로 통하는 문은 너무 작아서 나가려면 아기처럼 기어야 한다!

이런 이상한 특징들은 사람들이 매우 불편하게 느끼도록 만든다. 그들은 계속 균형을 잃고 때로는 넘어진다. 안에 10분만 있어도 현기증을 느끼게 하기에 충분하다! 그럼 그 예술가들은 왜 이런 별난 아파트를 만들었을까? 그들은 "집의 불편함은 당신이 좀 더 활동적으로 만들 거예요. 그것은 결국 당신을 더 건강하게 만들고 더 오래 살도록 도와줄 거예요!"라고 말했다. 그런데 그것은 효과가 있는가? 대답은 "그렇다!"이다. 한 남자는 여기서 2년 동안 살고 난 후 행복하다고 말한다. 그는 살이 빠졌고 더 건강하다고 느낀다.

discomfort[diskʌ́mfərt] 몡 불편 (comfort 몡 편안함 uncomfortable 혱 불편한) unique[juːníːk]
혱 독특한 reversible[rivə́ːrsəbl] 혱 거꾸로 할 수 있는 destiny[déstəni] 몡 운명 loft[lɔːft]
몡 다락방; *아파트 sphere[sfiər] 몡 구 cube[kjuːb] 몡 정육면체, 입방체 indoor[índɔːr]
혱 실내의 flat[flæt] 혱 평평한 bumpy[bʌ́mpi] 혱 울퉁불퉁한 unexpected[ʌ̀nikspéktid]
혱 예상치 못한, 뜻밖의 feel around 여기저기 더듬거리다 crawl[krɔːl] 동 기어가다
balance[bǽləns] 몡 균형 dizzy[dízi] 혱 어지러운 unusual[ʌnjúːʒuəl] 혱 특이한
[문제] latest[léitist] 혱 최신의 trend[trend] 몡 경향 smooth[smuːð] 혱 매끄러운
surface[sə́ːrfis] 몡 표면 have a hard time v-ing ···하느라 고생하다

구문 7행 The inside is **even** more surprising.
　　　　• even: '훨씬'의 의미로, 비교급을 강조하는 부사
　　　8행 The floors are **not** flat **but** bumpy like a chocolate chip cookie.
　　　　• not A but B: A가 아니라 B이다
　　　10행 Plus, the door to the veranda is **so** small **that** you have to crawl like a baby *to get out*!
　　　　• so … that ~: 너무 ···해서 ～하다
　　　　• to get out: '···하기 위해'라는 의미로, 목적을 나타내는 부사적 용법의 to부정사구
　　　15행 **Ten minutes** inside **is** enough to *make* you *feel* dizzy!
　　　　• Ten minutes: 시간, 거리, 가격, 무게 등은 단수 취급함
　　　　• 사역동사(make) + 목적어 + 동사원형: ···가 ～하게 하다
　　　19행 It will eventually make you healthier and **help** you **live** longer!
　　　　• help + 목적어 + 동사원형: ···가 ～하도록 돕다

STRATEGIC ORGANIZER　uncomfortable, colors, bumpy, find

EXPANDING KNOWLEDGE

1 various　**2** original　**3** equal　**4** identity

어휘　weird[wiərd] 혱 기이한　specific[spisífik] 혱 구체적인　equal[íːkwəl] 혱 동등한
personality[pə̀ːrsənǽləti] 몡 성격　identity[aidéntəti] 몡 독자성　absolute[ǽbsəlùːt] 혱 완전한, 완벽한　odd[ad] 혱 이상한, 특이한　peculiar[pikjúːljər] 혱 이상한, 별난
remarkable[rimɑ́ːrkəbl] 혱 놀라운, 주목할 만한　rare[rɛər] 혱 드문, 진기한
typical[típikəl] 혱 전형적인　common[kámən] 혱 흔한　ordinary[ɔ́ːrdənèri] 혱 보통의
[문제] quantity[kwántəti] 몡 양　quality[kwáləti] 몡 질; *특성, 특색

VOCABULARY REVIEW

A　**1** odd　**2** destiny　**3** crawl　**4** bumpy
B　**1** c　**2** d　　　C　**1** b　**2** c　**3** a　**4** d

unit 14 **CULTURE**　　　pp. 60-63

★*The Living Library*

1 d　**2** d　**3** We can learn who they really are and eventually break our prejudices.　**4** d　**5** b
6 *1)* F　*2)* T

요즘, 우리는 도서관에서 많은 것들을 할 수 있다. 우리는 인터넷을 사용하고, 음반을 빌리고, 심지어 수업도 들을 수 있다! 하지만 사람을 빌릴 수 있는 도서관이 있다는 것을 알고 있었는가? 그것은 살아있는 도서관이라고 불린다!

살아있는 도서관은 2000년에 덴마크에서 설립되었다. 현재 전 세계에는 많은 살아있는 도서관들이 있다! 이 도서관들이 사람들에게 빌려주는 것은 종종 <u>오해를 받는</u> 사람들인 '살아있는 책들'이다. 몇 가지 예는 버스 운전사와 페미니스트들인데, 그들은 종종 공격적이라고 여겨진다. 또 다른 예는 채식주의자들인데, 그들은 예민하다고 여겨진다. 도서관 이용자들이 살아있는 책을 빌리면, 그들은 그 사람과 30분 동안 대화할 수 있다.

그럼 왜 이런 독특한 도서관이 만들어졌을까? 살아있는 도서관의 설립자인 Ronni Abergel에 따르면, 우리는 종종 특정 사람들에게 부정적인 편견을 가지고 있다. 우리가 그들과 이야기하는 데 얼마간의 시간만 보낸다면, 우리는 그들이 정말 누구인지 알 수 있고 결국 우리의 편견을 깰 수 있다!

살아있는 도서관에서, 우리는 이것을 경험할 수 있다. 예를 들어, 사람들은 프로게이머들이 게임에 중독되었다고 생각하는 경향이 있다. 하지만 만일 당신이 실제로 프로게이머와 대화하며 시간을 보낸다면, 당신은 그가 중독된 것이 아니라는 것을 깨닫게 될 수도 있다. 어쩌면 그는 단지 자신의 일을 잘하기 위해서 게임을 하는 연습을 많이 하는 것뿐일지도 모른다. 이런 식으로, 살아있는 도서관은 우리에게 중요한 교훈을 가르쳐 준다. <u>표지만 보고 책을 판단하지 마라.</u>

어휘   library[láibrèri] 명 도서관   borrow[bárou] 동 빌리다, 대출하다   found[faund] 동 설립하다
(founder 명 창립자, 설립자)   lend[lend] 동 빌려주다   feminist[fémənist] 명 페미니스트,
남녀평등주의자   aggressive[əgrésiv] 형 공격적인   vegetarian[vèdʒətέəriən] 명 채식주의자
sensitive[sénsətiv] 형 섬세한; *예민한   negative[négətiv] 형 부정적인   prejudice[prédʒudis]
명 편견   addicted[ədíktid] 형 중독된 (addiction 명 중독)   [문제] respect[rispékt] 동 존경하다
misunderstand[mìsʌndərstǽnd] 동 오해하다

구문   2행   But, did you know (that) **there's** a library [*where* you can borrow a person]?
             • there's 앞에 동사 know의 목적절을 이끄는 접속사 that이 생략되어 있음
             • where 이하는 a library를 수식하는 관계부사절
       5행   **What** these libraries lend people are "living books" ….
             • what: '…하는 것'의 의미로, 선행사를 포함하는 관계대명사
       7행   … bus drivers and feminists, **who** are often considered aggressive.
             • who: bus drivers and feminists를 보충 설명하는 계속적 용법의 주격 관계대명사
       13행 If we just **spend some time talking** to them, we can learn [*who* they really are] …!
             • spend + 시간 + v-ing: …하는 데 (시간)을 보내다
             • who 이하는 '의문사 + 주어 + 동사' 어순의 간접의문문으로, 동사 learn의 목적어 역할을 함
       16행 But, **if** you actually **spent** time talking to a pro gamer, you **might realize** ….
             • If + 주어 + 동사의 과거형, 주어 + 조동사의 과거형 + 동사원형: 가정법 과거

STRATEGIC ORGANIZER   borrow, talk, misunderstood, prejudices

EXPANDING KNOWLEDGE

1 optimistic   **2** pessimistic   **3** subjective   **4** critical

어휘   viewpoint[vjú:pɔ̀int] 명 관점   objective[əbdʒéktiv] 형 객관적인
subjective[səbdʒéktiv] 형 주관적인   optimistic[àptəmístik] 형 낙관적인
pessimistic[pèsəmístik] 형 비관적인   bias[báiəs] 명 편견   angle[ǽŋgl] 명 각도; *시각, 관점
outlook[áutlùk] 명 관점   perspective[pərspéktiv] 명 관점, 시각
standpoint[stǽndpɔ̀int] 명 견지, 관점   critical[krítikəl] 형 비판적인
narrow[nǽrou] 형 (관점이) 좁은, 편협한   [문제] expect[ikspékt] 동 기대하다
belief[bilí:f] 명 믿음, 생각

unit 15 JOBS

pp. 64-67

Training Sea Mammals

1 c **2** c **3** a **4** c **5** It must be given at the exact moment when they perform it   **6** h

---

Sea World의 바다 포유동물 조련사인 Richard Maddox 씨가 우리에게 그의 직업에 대해 이야기해 주시겠습니다.

Q: 바다 포유동물 조련사는 무슨 일을 하나요?

A: 제 일은 기본적으로 바다 포유동물들을 훈련시키는 것입니다. 여러분은 아마도 돌고래가 공중으로 뛰어오르고, 고래가 지느러미를 흔들어 인사를 하고, 물개가 춤을 추는 것을 본 적이 있을 것입니다. 그것이 우리가 그들에게 하도록 가르치는 것입니다. 그러나 주로, 우리는 동물들을 돌봅니다. 우리는 그들의 음식을 준비하고, 그들의 수조를 청소하고, 그들의 건강을 관리합니다. 때로는 우리가 그들을 돌보는 것을 돕도록 그들을 훈련시킵니다. 예를 들어, 동물들은 혈액 샘플을 채취하거나 엑스레이를 촬영하는 것과 같은 의료시술을 받는 동안 가만히 있도록 배웁니다.

Q: 당신은 어떻게 동물들을 훈련시키나요?

A: 우리는 작은 단계들을 이용해서 그들에게 묘기를 가르칩니다. 예를 들면, 돌고래들을 뛰어오르게 하기 위해서, 우리는 먼저 그들이 수면 위의 빨간 공 같은 목표물을 건드리도록 가르칩니다. 그러고 나서, 우리는 목표물을 위로 올리기 시작합니다. 우리는 그들이 수면 위로 18피트 높이에 있는 목표물을 칠 수 있을 정도로 충분히 높이 뛰어오를 때까지 그 과정을 몇 번이고 반복합니다.

Q: 동물들에게 당신이 원하는 것을 하도록 가르치는 비결이 무엇인가요?

A: 보상을 주는 것이 매우 효과가 있습니다. 우리는 동물들에게 음식과 장난감을 주거나, '좋아'라고 말을 하거나, 그들을 쓰다듬어 주는 것으로 보상합니다. 그러나 어떤 행동을 가르치려면, 보상은 그들이 그것을 행하는 정확한 시점에 주어져야 합니다.

Q: 당신은 당신의 직업을 좋아하나요?

A: 물론 좋아합니다! 동물들을 훈련시키고 돌보는 것은 힘들지만 매우 보람 있습니다. 저는 제가 그들의 선생님이자, 부모이고, 최고의 친구라고 자랑스럽게 말할 수 있습니다!

어휘 mammal[mǽməl] 명 포유동물   trainer[tréinər] 명 훈련자; 조련사 (train 동 훈련하다)
basically[béisikəli] 부 기본적으로   dolphin[dálfin] 명 돌고래   whale[hweil] 명 고래
wave[weiv] 동 (손·팔을) 흔든다   seal[si:l] 명 바다표범, 물개   take care of …을 돌보다
tank[tæŋk] 명 탱크; *물통   monitor[mánətər] 동 감시하다, 관리하다   still[stil] 형 가만히 있는
medical[médikəl] 형 의학의   procedure[prəsí:dʒər] 명 절차; *수술, 시술   trick[trik] 명 속임수;
*재주, 곡예   target[tá:rgit] 명 목표; *목표물   surface[sə́:rfis] 명 표면, 수면   raise[reiz] 동 들어
올리다   repeat[ripí:t] 동 반복하다   reward[riwɔ́:rd] 명 보상 동 보상하다 (rewarding 형 보람 있는)
rub[rʌb] 동 문지르다; *쓰다듬다   care for …을 보살피다, 돌보다   proudly[práudli] 부 자랑스럽게
[문제] signal[sígnəl] 명 신호   responsible[rispánsəbl] 형 책임이 있는   checkup[tʃékʌ̀p]
명 건강진단

구문 4행   You've probably **seen** dolphins *jump* into the air, whales *wave* hello, and seals *dance*.
• have seen: '…한 적이 있다'라는 의미로, 경험을 나타내는 현재완료

- 지각동사(see) + 목적어 + 동사원형: …가 ～하는 것을 보다

5행 That's **what** we teach them to do.

- what: '…하는 것'의 의미로, 선행사를 포함하는 관계대명사

15행 … until they jump high **enough to hit** the target 18 feet above the surface.

- enough to-v: …할 정도로 충분히

20행 But **for an action** *to be taught*, the reward must be given at the exact moment [**when** they perform it].

- for an action: to부정사의 의미상 주어
- to be taught: '…하려면'의 의미로, 조건을 나타내는 부사적 용법의 to부정사구
- when 이하는 the exact moment를 수식하는 관계부사절

STRATEGIC ORGANIZER tanks, tricks, rewards, rubbing

EXPANDING KNOWLEDGE

1 *1)* tail *2)* threat *3)* pollution   **2** *1)* F *2)* T

어휘 classification[klæsəfikéiʃən] 몡 분류   sea lion 바다사자   walrus[wɔ́ːlrəs] 몡 바다코끼리
sea cow 바다소   polar bear 북극곰   otter[átər] 몡 수달   tail[teil] 몡 꼬리
fin[fin] 몡 지느러미   fur[fəːr] 몡 털   habitat[hǽbitæt] 몡 서식지   coastal[kóustəl] 혱 해안의
threat[θret] 몡 협박, 위협   hunting[hʌ́ntiŋ] 몡 사냥   competition[kàmpətíʃən] 몡 경쟁
pollution[pəlúːʃən] 몡 오염   global warming 지구온난화

VOCABULARY REVIEW

A **1** prepare **2** repeat **3** reward **4** mammal
B **1** d **2** a   C **1** a **2** d **3** b **4** c

unit 16 TECHNOLOGY

pp. 68-71

★*Ubiquitous Healthcare*

1 b **2** get proper medical care anywhere and anytime **3** b **4** d **5** d **6** *1)* F *2)* T

아프면, 당신은 병원에 간다. 하지만 만약 당신이 병원이 없는 시골 지역에 산다면, 의사를 찾아가는 것은 쉽지 않다. 하지만 새롭게 개발된 네트워킹 기술 덕분에, 당신은 언제 어디에서나 적절한 건강 관리를 받을 수 있다. 이 기술은 유비쿼터스 의료 서비스이며, U-health라고도 알려져 있다.

환자들이 이 서비스를 이용하기 위해서는, 일상생활에서 손목, 가슴, 허리를 포함한 다양한 신체 부위에 센서를 착용해야 한다. (어떤 환자들은 센서를 착용하는 것이 불편하다고 불평한다.) 그 센서들은 정기적으로 체온과 심장 박동, 그리고 혈압과 같은 중요한 자료를 수집한다. 이 수집된 자료는 무선 네트워킹 시스템을 통해서 의료 서비스 센터에 보내진다. 만약 심각한 변화가 감지되면, 그 시스템은 의사에게 경고를 보낼 것이다. 그러면 의사들은 환자의 건강 상태를 알아보기 위해 자료를 검토하고, 치료법이나 심지어 식단의 변화까지 제안한다. 이것은 직접 의사를 방문하는 것과 똑같다!

그러므로 이 시스템은 병원에 가기 위해 먼 거리를 쉽게 이동할 수 없는 나이 든 사람들에게 도움이 될 수 있다. 게다가, 그것은 사람들이 간단한 건강진단을 받는 데 소비하는 시간과 돈을 절약해준다.

U-health는 여전히 새롭고 개발 중인 기술이지만, 가까운 미래에는 사람들이 더 이상 병원에 갈 필요가 없을지도 모른다. U-health 시스템으로 의사가 당신에게 찾아올 것이다!

rural[rúərəl] 형 시골의, 지방의   thanks to … 덕분에   develop[divéləp] 통 발달시키다; *개발하다
technology[teknálədʒi] 명 기술   proper[prápər] 형 적절한   medical care 의료, 건강 관리
sensor[sénsər] 명 센서, 감지기   wrist[rist] 명 손목   chest[tʃest] 명 가슴   waist[weist] 명 허리
complain[kəmpléin] 통 불평하다   regularly[régjulərli] 부 정기적으로, 규칙적으로
collect[kəlékt] 통 수집하다   temperature[témpərətʃər] 명 온도; *체온
heartbeat[háːrtbìːt] 명 심장 박동   blood pressure 혈압   wireless[wáiərlis] 형 무선의
detect[ditékt] 통 발견하다, 감지하다   alert[ələ́ːrt] 명 경계; *경고   suggest[səgdʒést] 통 제안하다
treatment[tríːtmənt] 명 취급; *치료(법)   diet[dáiət] 명 식이요법   distance[dístəns] 명 거리
[문제] welfare[wélfɛər] 명 복지, 행복   elderly[éldərli] 형 연세가 드신   in person 직접, 스스로

구문   4행   This technology is Ubiquitous Healthcare, (which is) **also known** as U-Health.
　• also known 앞에 '주격 관계대명사 + be동사'가 생략되어 있음

5행   **For patients** *to use* this service, they need to wear sensors on ….
　• For patients: to부정사의 의미상 주어
　• to use: '…하기 위해'라는 의미로, 목적을 나타내는 부사적 용법의 to부정사

14행   Therefore, this system can be helpful for older people [**who** are not able to …].
　• who 이하는 older people을 수식하는 주격 관계대명사절

15행   In addition, it saves the time and money [**that** people spend to get a simple medical checkup].
　• that 이하는 the time and money를 수식하는 목적격 관계대명사절

STRATEGIC ORGANIZER   medical, sensors, suggestions, cheaper

EXPANDING KNOWLEDGE

1 *1)* transfer *2)* satellite *3)* signal   **2** *1)* F *2)* T

어휘   communication[kəmjùːnəkéiʃən] 명 의사소통, 연락   transmitter[trænsmítər] 명 송신기, 발신기
receiver[risíːvər] 명 수화기, 수신기   radio[réidiòu] 형 무선의, 무전의   electromagnetic
[ilèktroumægnétik] 형 전자기의   fidelity[fidéləti] 명 정확도, 충실도   Global Positioning
System(GPS) 위성 위치 확인 시스템   satellite[sætəlàit] 형 위성의   application[æpləkéiʃən]
명 적용, 응용   mobile[móubəl] 형 이동하는, 이동식의   transfer[trǽnsfər] 명 이동   device[diváis]
명 장치, 기구   [문제] orbit[ɔ́ːrbit] 통 (지구 등의) 궤도를 돌다   wave[weiv] 명 파도; *파장, 파동
accessible[əksésəbl] 형 이용 가능한   wired[wáiərd] 형 유선의

VOCABULARY REVIEW

A *1* rural *2* temperature *3* complain *4* sensor
B *1* c *2* b   **C** *1* b *2* c *3* d *4* c

unit 17 PSYCHOLOGY   pp. 72-75

False Memories

1 a **2** b **3** Because Bugs Bunny is not a Disney character. **4** *1)* b *2)* c *3)* a **5** d **6** *1)* T *2)* F

우리의 기억은 우리가 보고, 듣고, 경험한 것으로부터 형성된다. 하지만 때때로, 사람들은 실제로는 절대로 일어나지 않은 일들이나 사건들을 기억한다. 이것은 거짓 기억이라 불린다. 그것은 어떻게 일어나는 것인가?

Elizabeth Loftus라는 한 심리학자가 알아내기 위해 실험을 실시했다. 그 실험에서, 연구자들은 디즈니랜드에 대한 가짜 광고를 만들었다. 그것은 그곳에서 사람들과 악수를 하고 있는 벅스버니라는 만화 캐릭터를 보여주었다. 그것을 보고 난 후, 참가자들은 그들이 어렸을 때 디즈니랜드에서 벅스버니를 만났던 것을 기억하는지 질문을 받았다. 약 35퍼센트의 사람들이 그렇다고 대답했다. 더구나, 그들 중 몇몇은 그와 포옹한 일이나 사진을 찍은 일과 같은 세부적인 일들을 기억할 수 있다고 말했다. 하지만 벅스버니는 디즈니의 캐릭터가 아니기 때문에 이것은 불가능하다!

그러면 어떻게 이런 거짓 기억들이 만들어지는가? 연구에 따르면, 거짓 기억들은 우리의 실제 기억들과 거짓 암시들이 결합되면서 쉽게 만들어진다. 사람들에게 디즈니랜드에서 벅스버니를 만난 일과 같은 거짓 정보가 주어지면, 그들은 마음속으로 그 상황을 상상한다. 후에, 그들이 상상한 것은 디즈니랜드를 방문한 것과 같은 그들의 실제 기억들과 섞인다. 그리고 나면 실제 사건의 기억과 암시된 사건의 기억을 구별하기 어려워진다. 결국, 사람들은 그들이 암시된 사건을 정말로 경험했다고 믿고, 거짓 기억을 만들어 낸다.

사실, 거짓 기억은 거짓말을 하는 것과 같지 않다. 거짓인 것은 단지 그 기억일 뿐이다. 그렇다면 당신 자신의 기억에 대해 생각해 봐라. 그것들 모두가 진짜라고 확신하는가?

어휘 form[fɔːrm] 통 형성하다　experience[ikspíəriəns] 통 경험하다　actually[ǽktʃuəli] 부 실제로 (actual 형 실제의)　false[fɔːls] 형 틀린, 사실이 아닌　psychologist[saikálədʒist] 명 심리학자　carry out …을 수행하다　experiment[ikspérəmənt] 명 실험　fake[feik] 형 가짜의, 거짓된　advertisement[ædvərtáizmənt] 명 광고　participant[pɑːrtísəpənt] 명 참가자　detail[ditéil] 명 세부사항　hug[hʌg] 통 껴안다　research[risə́ːrtʃ] 명 연구, 조사　combine[kəmbáin] 통 결합하다　suggestion[səgdʒéstʃən] 명 제안; *암시 (suggest 통 암시하다)　imagine[imǽdʒin] 통 상상하다 (imagination 명 상상)　situation[sìtʃuéiʃən] 명 상황, 처지　mix[miks] 통 섞다　distinguish[distíŋgwiʃ] 통 구별하다　[문제] shake hands with …와 악수하다　confusion[kənfjúːʒən] 명 혼동　claim[kleim] 통 주장하다

구문

1행　Our memory is formed from **what** we have seen, heard, and experienced.
　　• what: '…하는 것'의 의미로, 선행사를 포함하는 관계대명사

6행　It showed the cartoon character Bugs Bunny [**shaking** hands with people there].
　　• shaking 이하는 Bugs Bunny를 수식하는 현재분사구

6행　After seeing it, the participants were asked **if** they *remembered meeting* Bugs Bunny ….
　　• if: '…인지 (아닌지)'라는 의미의 접속사
　　• remember v-ing: (과거에) …한 것을 기억하다

17행　And then **it** becomes hard [**to *distinguish*** memories of real events *from* memories of the suggested ones].
　　• it은 가주어이고, to distinguish 이하가 진주어
　　• distinguish A from B: A와 B를 구별하다

20행　**It's** just the memory **that** is false.
　　• It is … that ~: '~한 것은 바로 …이다'의 의미로, the memory를 강조하는 강조구문

STRATEGIC SUMMARY　false, combines, suggested, believed

EXPANDING KNOWLEDGE

1　1) function　2) injury　3) disorder　　**2**　1) T　2) T

어휘 function[fʌ́ŋkʃən] 명 기능　store[stɔːr] 통 저장하다　recall[rikɔ́ːl] 통 기억해내다　short-term[ʃɔ́ːrttə̀ːrm] 형 단기의　long-term[lɔ́ːŋtə̀ːrm] 형 장기의　factor[fǽktər] 명 요소　odor[óudər] 명 냄새　previous[príːviəs] 형 이전의　disorder[disɔ́ːrdər] 명 (신체 기능의) 장애　injury[índʒəri] 명 부상, 상처　aging[éidʒiŋ] 명 노화　reduction[ridʌ́kʃən] 명 감소　[문제] illness[ílnis] 명 병　influence[ínfluəns] 통 영향을 미치다　fitness[fítnis] 명 건강

VOCABULARY REVIEW
A **1** combine **2** memory **3** detail **4** participant
B **1** d **2** b   C **1** b **2** c **3** a **4** d

★unit★ 18 HEALTH

pp. 76-79

★Superfoods

1 a **2** d **3** c **4** They can protect us from cancer and improve our vision. **5** b **6** d

시금치, 호박, 토마토, 블루베리 등. 이 평범한 과일과 채소들은 모두 공통점을 가지고 있다. 그것들은 슈퍼푸드라는 것이다! 대부분의 슈퍼푸드는 밝은 빛깔을 가진 과일과 채소이다. 게다가, 연어와 같은 특정한 생선과 호두와 같은 견과류 역시 이러한 종류의 음식에 포함된다.

그렇다면 무엇이 이 음식들을 그렇게 '대단하게' 만들까? 그 용어를 처음 사용한 Steven Pratt 박사에 따르면, 이 음식들은 영양가가 매우 높아서 엄청난 건강상의 이득이 있다. 그것들은 우리에게 많은 활력을 주고 우리가 질병과 노화에 맞서 싸우도록 돕는다. 그리고 이 음식들은 건강에 좋을 뿐만 아니라 열량도 낮다. 그래서, 당신은 그것들을 규칙적으로 먹음으로써 심지어 체중도 감량할 수 있다.

뽀빠이가 가장 좋아하는 음식인 시금치는 최고의 슈퍼푸드 중 하나이다. 이것은 놀랍지 않은데, 왜냐하면 시금치에는 비타민 A, 비타민 C, 그리고 다양한 무기질이 많기 때문이다. 이들은 우리의 면역 체계를 강화한다. 한편, 블루베리에는 비타민 C와 항산화제가 많이 들어 있다. 이 영양분들은 우리를 암으로부터 보호해주고 시력을 향상할 수 있다. 그리고 연어는 높은 수치의 오메가 3 지방산을 함유하고 있는데, 이것은 심장병을 예방하도록 돕는다.

하지만, 모든 사람들이 슈퍼푸드라는 발상에 동의하는 것은 아니다. 일부 영양 전문가들은 이 음식들의 건강상의 이점들이 과대평가된다고 주장한다. (그래서 당신은 건강을 위해 슈퍼푸드를 더 많이 먹어야 한다.) 어떤 사람들은 또한 슈퍼푸드만 먹고 그 밖에 다른 것들은 먹지 않는 것이 좋지 않다고 경고한다. 슈퍼푸드가 아무리 건강에 좋을지라도, 항상 균형 잡힌 식사를 하는 것이 중요하다!

어휘　spinach[spínitʃ] 몡 시금치　pumpkin[pʌ́mpkin] 몡 호박　plain[plein] 혱 명백한; *평범한
have … in common (특징 등을) 공통적으로 지니다　salmon[sǽmən] 몡 연어　nut[nʌt] 몡 견과
walnut[wɔ́ːlnʌt] 몡 호두　include[inklúːd] 동 포함하다　term[təːrm] 몡 용어, 말
nutritious[njuːtríʃəs] 혱 영양분이 많은, 영양가가 높은 (nutrition 몡 영양(물) nutrient 몡 영양소,
영양분)　benefit[bénəfit] 몡 혜택, 이득　regularly[régjulərli] 閈 정기적으로, 규칙적으로
mineral[mínərəl] 몡 무기물　strengthen[stréŋkθən] 동 강화하다　immune system 면역 체계
meanwhile[míːnwàil] 閈 그 동안에; *한편　vision[víʒən] 몡 시력　contain[kəntéin]
동 …이 들어 있다, 함유되어 있다　fatty acid 지방산　overestimate[òuvəréstəmeit] 동 과대평가하다
balanced[bǽlənst] 혱 균형 잡힌　[문제] side effect 부작용

구문　8행　According to Dr. Steven Pratt, **who** first used the term, these foods are *so* highly
nutritious *that* they have great health benefits.
• who: Dr. Steven Pratt를 보충 설명하는 계속적 용법의 주격 관계대명사
• so … that ~: 너무 …해서 ~하다

19행　However, **not everyone** agrees with the idea of superfoods.
• not everyone: '모두가 …인 것은 아니다'라는 의미의 부분부정

22행　Some also warn [**that** *it*'s not good *to eat* only superfoods and nothing else].
• that: 동사 warn의 목적어인 명사절을 이끄는 접속사
• it은 가주어이고, to eat 이하가 진주어

23행 **No matter how healthy superfoods are**, it is important to always have a balanced diet!

- no matter how + 형용사 + 주어 + 동사: 아무리 …가 ~할지라도(= however + 형용사 + 주어 + 동사)

STRATEGIC ORGANIZER energetic, diseases, minerals, overvalued

EXPANDING KNOWLEDGE

1 *1)* deficiency   *2)* improper   *3)* obesity   **2** *1)* T   *2)* F

어휘   carbohydrate[kὰːrbouháidreit] 몡 탄수화물   protein[próutiːn] 몡 단백질   fat[fæt] 몡 지방
soluble[sάljubl] 몡 용해성이 있는   improper[imprάpər] 몡 부적절한   deficiency[difíʃənsi]
몡 결핍   starvation[staːrvéiʃən] 몡 굶주림   excess[iksés] 몡 과도, 과잉 (excessive 몡 과도한,
지나친)   obesity[oubíːsəti] 몡 비만   diabetes[dὰiəbíːtis] 몡 당뇨병   [문제] suitable[súːtəbl]
몡 적절한   particular[pərtíkjulər] 몡 특정한   severely[sivíərli] 뮏 심하게
overweight[óuvərwèit] 몡 과체중의   dissolve[dizάlv] 동 녹이다, 용해하다
consumption[kənsʌ́mpʃən] 몡 소비, 소모

VOCABULARY REVIEW

A *1* aging   *2* term   *3* nutritious   *4* immune system
B *1* d   *2* b   **C** *1* c   *2* b   *3* d   *4* d

19 SOCIETY

pp. 80-83

★*Oxfam*

1 a   **2** It was to collect food and clothes for families whose lives had been ruined by the war.
3 c   **4** b   **5** d   **6** *1)* F *2)* F

Oxfam이 무엇인지 아는가? 그 이름이 당신에게 황소 혹은 가족을 떠올리게 할지 몰라도, 그것은 그것들과 아무런 관련이 없다. 사실, Oxfam은 전 세계 90개가 넘는 국가에서 세계적인 빈곤에 맞서 싸우는 국제 조직이다.

'Oxfam'이라는 이름은 옥스퍼드 빈민 구호 위원회에서 비롯되었다. 그것은 제2차 세계 대전 중인 1942년에 한 집단의 옥스퍼드 시민들에 의해 설립되었다. 그것의 첫 임무는 전쟁으로 삶이 파괴된 가정들을 위해 식량과 의복을 모으는 것이었다.

요즘, Oxfam은 기근을 완화하기 위해 가난의 원인을 해결하는 것에 더 주력한다. 그 단체는 사람들에게 식량과 의복 제공 같은 단기적인 지원을 하는 것뿐만 아니라 그들에게 가난에서 벗어날 수 있는 장기적인 해결책을 제시함으로써 그들을 돕는다. 예를 들어, 그것은 더 나은 미래를 위해 가난한 아이들이 좋은 교육을 받도록 돕는다. 그것은 또한 소규모 사업을 시작할 수 있도록 가난한 사람들에게 자금을 대출해 주기도 한다.

게다가, Oxfam은 세계 전역에 상점들을 운영한다. 이 상점들은 기증받은 중고 제품들과 무엇보다도 개발도상국에서 만들어진 다양한 제품들을 판매한다. 수공예품, 의복, 장난감, 그리고 악기가 이에 속한다. 이러한 제품들은 그것들을 생산하는 공동체의 삶의 질을 향상하도록 돕기 위해 공정 거래를 통해 판매된다. 또한, 그 수익은 Oxfam의 구호활동에 자금을 대기 위해 사용된다.

어휘   ox[aks] 몡 황소   international[ìntərnǽʃənəl] 몡 국제적인   organization[ɔ̀rgənizéiʃən] 몡 조직,
단체   poverty[pάvərti] 몡 가난   committee[kəmíti] 몡 위원회   famine[fǽmin] 몡 기근
relief[rilíːf] 몡 안도; *구호 (relieve 동 완화하다, 줄이다)   mission[míʃən] 몡 임무, 사명

ruin[rúːin] 图 파괴하다   assistance[əsístəns] 圀 원조, 지원   escape[iskéip] 图 달아나다; *벗어나다
offer[ɔ́ːfər] 图 제공하다   loan[loun] 图 대출하다, (돈을) 빌려주다   secondhand[sékəndhǽnd]
圀 간접의; *중고의   goods[gudz] 圀 상품   developing country 개발도상국   boost[buːst]
图 신장시키다, 북돋우다   community[kəmjúːnəti] 圀 공동체, 지역 사회   profit[práfit] 圀 이익, 수익
[문제] consumer[kənsúːmər] 圀 소비자   practical[prǽktikəl] 圀 실질적인   financial[finǽnʃəl]
圀 재정의, 금융의   handicraft[hǽndikræft] 圀 수공예품   enable[inéibl] 图 …을 가능하게 하다
shelter[ʃéltər] 圀 피난처, 은신처

구문   1행   Although the name may **remind** you **of** an ox or a family, it *has nothing to do with* them.
 • remind A of B: A에게 B를 상기시키다
 • have nothing to do with: …와 관계가 없다

10행   Its first mission was **to collect** food and clothes for families [*whose* lives **had been ruined** by the war].
 • to collect: 주격 보어로 쓰인 명사적 용법의 to부정사
 • whose 이하는 families를 수식하는 소유격 관계대명사절
 • had been ruined: 주절의 시제보다 앞선 시점의 내용을 가리키는 과거완료 수동태

13행   …, Oxfam focuses more on [**solving** the causes of poverty] *to relieve* famine.
 • solving 이하는 전치사 on의 목적어 역할을 하는 동명사구
 • to relieve: '…하기 위해'라는 의미로, 목적을 나타내는 부사적 용법의 to부정사

18행   …, but also by offering them long-term solutions **to escape** poverty.
 • to escape: long-term solutions를 수식하는 형용사적 용법의 to부정사

23행   …, more importantly, a variety of products [**made** in developing countries].
 • made 이하는 a variety of products를 수식하는 과거분사구

STRATEGIC ORGANIZER   poverty, relieve, causes, developing

EXPANDING KNOWLEDGE

1 *1)* shortage *2)* disaster *3)* drought   **2** *1)* F *2)* T

어휘   drought[draut] 圀 가뭄   shortage[ʃɔ́ːrtiʤ] 圀 부족   government[gʌ́vərnmənt]
圀 정부   policy[páləsi] 圀 정책   disaster[dizǽstər] 圀 재난, 재해   market crash 시장 붕괴
biological[bàiəládʒikəl] 圀 생물학적인   malnutrition[mæ̀lnjuːtríʃn] 圀 영양실조
breakdown[bréikdàun] 圀 고장; *(시스템 등의) 실패, 와해   structure[strʌ́ktʃər] 圀 구조
migration[maigréiʃən] 圀 이주, 이동   [문제] man-made[mǽnméid] 圀 사람이 만든, 인공의

VOCABULARY REVIEW

A **1** assistance **2** poverty **3** run **4** loan
B **1** a **2** c   **C** **1** c **2** d **3** b **4** a

★unit★
20 ENVIRONMENT   pp. 84-87

★*Carbon Trading*

1 d **2** b **3** b, c **4** It gives companies time to reduce their emissions slowly. **5** b **6** *1)* F *2)* F

지구 온난화는 심각한 문제가 되고 있다. 그것의 주요 원인 중 하나는 이산화탄소의 배출이다. 이 문제를 해결하기 위해, 현재 '탄소 거래'가 이용되고 있다.

탄소 거래는 1997년에 교토 의정서로 시작되었다. 이 협정에 따르면, 각 국가는 배출에 대한 국가 허용치를 부여받는다. 그러면 정부는 회사들에 '탄소 배출권'을 준다. 한 회사가 받는 배출권의 수는 회사의 크기와 사업 분야에 따라 결정된다. 한 회사가 탄소를 덜 배출해서 배출권 모두를 사용하지 않으면, 그 회사는 남은 배출권을 거래해서 돈을 벌 수 있다. 하지만 회사들은 시간이 갈수록 배출량을 줄여야 하는데, 왜냐하면 허용치가 매년 낮아지기 때문이다.

탄소 거래는 회사들이 그것으로부터 돈을 벌 수 있어 배출량을 줄이기 위해 더 열심히 노력할 가능성이 있다는 점에서 좋다. 또한, 그것은 갑작스러운 경제적 어려움을 막기 위해 회사들에 배출량을 천천히 줄일 시간을 준다. 하지만 몇 가지 문제들도 있다. 우선 첫째로, 회사들은 계속해서 오염을 일으킬 수 있다. 뿐만 아니라, 어떤 경우에는 허용치가 너무 높아서 아무런 거래가 일어나지 않는다.

이러한 단점들에도 불구하고, 영국은 이제 가정을 대상으로 비슷한 제도를 고려하고 있다. 이 제도하에서, 가정들은 다른 가정들과 배출권을 거래할 수 있을 것이다. 당신은 이것이 좋은 아이디어라고 생각하는가?

어휘 emission[imíʃən] 몡 배출(물) (emit 동 배출하다) carbon dioxide 이산화탄소 trading[tréidiŋ] 몡 거래 (trade 동 거래하다) protocol[próutəkɔ̀:l] 몡 의정서, 조약안 agreement[əgrí:mənt] 몡 협정 national[nǽʃənl] 형 국가의 limit[límit] 몡 한계; *제한, 허용치 depend on …에 달려 있다, …에 의해 결정되다 area[ɛ́əriə] 몡 지역; *분야 remaining[riméiniŋ] 형 남아 있는 cut[kʌt] 동 자르다; *줄이다 lower[lóuər] 동 내리다, 낮추다 reduce[ridjú:s] 동 줄이다 economic[èkənámik] 형 경제의 take place 일어나다 disadvantage[dìsədvǽntidʒ] 몡 불리한 점, 약점 household[háushòuld] 몡 가정 [문제] carbon credit 탄소 배출권 industry[índəstri] 몡 산업 despite[dispáit] 전 …에도 불구하고 apply[əplái] 동 신청하다; *적용하다

구문 6행 **The number of credits** [(which[that]) *a company* gets] **depends** on ….
• the number of + 복수명사: '…의 수'라는 의미로, 단수 취급함
• a company 앞에 the number of credits를 선행사로 하는 목적격 관계대명사가 생략되어 있음

11행 Carbon trading is good **in that** companies can make money from it, so they *are likely to try* harder ….
• in that: …라는 점에서, …이므로
• be likely to-v: …할 것 같다

15행 Furthermore, in some cases limits are **so** high **that** no trading takes place.
• so … that ~: 너무 …해서 ~하다

STRATEGIC SUMMARY   trade, economic, polluting, occurs

EXPANDING KNOWLEDGE

1 international   **2** loss   **3** import   **4** profit

어휘 export[ikspɔ́:rt] 동 수출하다 몡 수출 import[impɔ́:rt] 동 수입하다 몡 수입 loss[lɔ:s] 몡 손실; 손실액 (lose 동 잃다) demand[dimǽnd] 몡 수요 supply[səplái] 몡 공급 exchange[ikstʃéindʒ] 몡 교환 동 교환하다 deal[di:l] 몡 거래 동 거래하다 contract[kántrækt] 몡 계약 동 계약하다 barter[bá:rtər] 몡 물물교환 동 물건을 교환하다 fair[fɛər] 몡 박람회 형 공정한 barrier[bǽriər] 몡 장애물, 장벽 promote[prəmóut] 동 촉진하다

VOCABULARY REVIEW

A **1** trading **2** emission **3** lower **4** cause
B **1** b **2** c   C **1** a **2** d **3** b **4** c

MEMO

MEMO

MEMO